Laity
American and Catholic
Transforming the Church

William V. D'Antonio, James D. Davidson,
Dean R. Hoge and Ruth A. Wallace

Sheed & Ward
Kansas City

Sheed & Ward™ is a service of The National Catholic Reporter Publishing Company.

Library of Congress Cataloguing-in-Publication Data

Laity, American and Catholic : transforming the Church / William V. D'Antonio . . . [et al.].
p. cm.
Includes bibliographical references and index.
ISBN: 1-55612-823-1 (alk. paper)
1. Catholic Church--United States--History--1965- 2. Laity--Catholic Church--Statistics. 3. Laity--United States--Statistics. 4. Catholic Church--Public opinion. 5. Public opinion--United States. I. D'Antonio, William V.
BX1406.2.L295 1995
282'.73'09045--dc20 95-48857
CIP

Published by: Sheed & Ward
115 E. Armour Blvd.
P.O. Box 419492
Kansas City, MO 64141-6492

To order, call: (800) 333-7373

Contents

In Memoriam

Joseph H. Fichter, SJ

Preface

THERE HAVE BEEN MANY DEVELOPMENTS IN THE PERIOD SINCE THE close of the Second Vatican Council in 1965. Some trends are clearly signs of hope and long-term viability in the Church; others point to problems which might contribute to organizational decline. The hopeful signs include continued growth in the number of Catholics, up from about 40 million in 1960 to about 60 million in 1992; an increase in the number of Catholic parishes – 20,000 in 1992, compared to 17,000 in 1960; growing numbers of teachers in Catholic schools, resulting in a better teacher-student ratio (down from one teacher per 28 students in 1960 to one for every 16 students today); a doubling in the number of students enrolled in Catholic colleges and universities (from about 300,000 in 1960 to about 650,000 in 1992); and, growing indications that Catholic lay people want to play larger roles in their parishes and want to collaborate with clergy in formulating policies which affect the laity's lives most directly.

At the same time, there are many areas of concern. As nearly everyone knows by now, there have been sharp declines in the number of priests and sisters, and as Schoenherr and Young (1993) indicate, these trends are likely to continue; Catholics' financial contributions to the Church (now only about one percent of Catholics' incomes) are the lowest of any major faith group (Greeley and McManus, 1987; Hoge, *et al*, 1994); as we will show, clergy and lay people alike are concerned about the quality of religious education young Catholics are receiving; some people are very concerned about the younger generation's willingness to support the Church in the future; there seem to be growing tensions between the hierarchy and lay people over issues such as the ordination of women and optional celibacy; there continue to be important divisions over sexual ethics; and concerns seem to be growing about the role that the Church's largest ethnic group – Latinos – will play in the Church in the years ahead.

In this book we examine both kinds of changes – those which point to the enduring strengths of the Church, and those which are problematic. We review trends in the laity's attitudes and behaviors during the 30 years since Vatican II and, especially, since our 1989 volume *American Catholic Laity in a Changing Church.* Before we get into specific findings, we want to provide some background.

This book is a sequel to our 1987 survey of American Catholics that resulted in the book *American Catholic Laity in a Changing Church.* As with the first book, it emerged from discussions between the co-authors and the *National Catholic Reporter* publisher, William McSweeney, and its editor, Tom Fox. Everyone agreed that the period since the publication of the earlier work had seen so many important events that a six-year follow-up should produce trend data important to the readership of the NCR and to the larger public.

The National Catholic Reporter Publishing Company generously provided the funds, and the co-authors again contracted with the Gallup Organization for a survey of American Catholics. The survey was carried out in the same period of the spring (April and May) as the earlier survey. Gallup pollers conducted 20-minute interviews using the system of random digit dialing, with 802 completed interviews of Catholics in non-institutionalized settings, aged 18 and over. The interview form appears in the Appendix.

We repeated most of the questions used in 1987, deleting only those few that seemed no longer relevant, thus making available space to add new questions. Our major objective was to carry out a trend analysis, to find out just how much the Catholic laity might have changed in these six years, and in which direction.

The reader will recall that during these six years, the abortion issue became more and more central both within the American political sphere and within the Church. The pope spoke out against abortion on numerous occasions and the U.S. bishops did also; with funds from the Knights of Columbus, the bishops hired a public relations firm to help promote their pro-life/anti-abortion campaign. This was also the period during which stories of sexual abuse by priests of Catholics of all ages received banner headlines. And it was a period during which more and more lay Catholic groups began to speak out, to question the highly controlled, centralized model of Church being reasserted by Pope John Paul II. But it was also a time when the Pope called us to work for peace, to protect the environment, to promote greater interfaith understanding, and to end all forms of anti-Semitism. He came to the United States to address a rally of more than 150,000 young people in Denver, where he called Americans to be more sensitive to the needs of young people. He continued to be praised for his moral stands, even as he was criticized for his autocratic style.

Our study focuses on questions of individual freedom vs. obedience to church leaders, the locus of moral authority, and democratic vs. autocratic decision-making in the Roman Catholic Church over the six year period 1987-1993. At the same time we have placed our study in the broader context of the struggle between the Americanist / integrationist and the Europeanist / restorationist conception of the Church that festered during the last third of the 19th and the early part of the 20th centuries. But the struggle now is being played out in the aftermath of Vatican II, and with a laity much more educated and sophisticated than ever.

For many of the laity the documents of Vatican II signaled a new era in Church history, an era that would include not only the bishops in closer dialogue with the Vatican on matters of Church teachings, but would include the laity also. Support for this belief is found in Chapter 12 of *Lumen Gentium* (Light of all Nations), one of Vatican II's important documents. The statement says in part, "The body of the faithful as a whole, anointed as they are by the Holy One" (Cf. Jn. 2:20, 27) cannot err in matters of belief. Thanks to a supernatural sense of the faith which characterizes the People as a whole, it manifests this unerring quality when, "from the bishops down to the last member of the laity, it shows universal agreement in matters of faith and morals."[1] Our data suggest that one way to move toward this universal agreement is for more open dialogue and interaction between the bishops and the laity.

While the main body of data to be used in this book comes from the 1987 and 1993 surveys, we also rely on several other surveys. For example, two of the co-authors helped construct a 1992 survey for Catholics Speak Out, also carried out by the Gallup Organization. In the text that survey will be referred to as the 1992 survey.

William D'Antonio also analyzed the data from a 1993 survey carried out for Catholics for a Free Choice by the KRC Research and Consulting Firm of New York City. When data from that survey are used, the reference will be to the CFFC 1993 survey. James Davidson and other members of his Catholic Pluralism Project have conducted individual interviews and focus groups with Catholics in Indiana. They also have conducted a statewide survey of over 4,600 members of 49 parishes. Some of their findings are reported in Chapters 4 and 5.

1. See p. 29 of *The Documents of Vatican II*. 1966. Walter M. Abbott, S.J. (general editor). Herder and Herder Association Press.

Wallace used data from Hoge's 1985 *The Future of Catholic Leadership* and the 1994 *Los Angeles Times* Surveys of Roman Catholic Priests and Nuns in the United States. These surveys will be referred to by their respective dates. Other surveys used in this book are cited as they appear in the text. In Chapter 2, we provide a statement in the footnotes about use of statistics throughout the book.

We are grateful to the following colleagues for their critical readings of some or all of the manuscript: Charlie Davis, Denise Shannon, Brother Cyprian Rowe, and James Coriden. We also wish to thank three anonymous readers for their critiques as well as their encouragement and help. To William McSweeney, Jr. and Tom Fox of the *National Catholic Reporter,* and Robert Heyer, Editor-in-Chief of Sheed & Ward, we owe a special debt of gratitude for their continued support of our work. To the Gallup Organization, our thanks for carrying out the two surveys for us in a timely fashion. To Betty Seaver, an old friend, we are grateful for blending our different styles into a readable manuscript. And to Monica Widmaier, we owe a special word of thanks for transferring chapters and tables from a variety of computer disks, getting them properly formatted, spell-checked, and finally producing a clean copy with everything in place. We thank all those anonymous persons who participated in the surveys for being willing to share their beliefs and attitudes with us. We alone are responsible for the result.

We are also grateful to a large number of colleagues in the sociology of religion with whom we have worked, collaborated and discussed these issues of tension, change, conflict and persistence over more than a generation. In this regard, we wish to express a special word of gratitude to the Rev. Joseph H. Fichter, S.J., whose death during the past year has deprived us of a close friend and smiling critic. By his example he inspired and motivated a generation of sociologists. In dedicating this book to his memory, we are acknowledging his encouragement and support, and trust that his spirit will be forgiving if our efforts fall short of his expectations.

William V. D'Antonio, Adjunct Research Professor, Catholic University, is currently working on a Lilly grant to study Small Christian Communities within the Catholic Church in the United States. James D. Davidson, Professor of Sociology at Purdue University, is directing the Catholic Pluralism Project, a national study of Catholics' religious beliefs and practices. Dean Hoge, Professor of Sociology, Catholic University, is the award-winning co-author of *Vanishing Boundaries*, a study of Baby Boomers in Protestant churches. And Ruth

Wallace, Professor of Sociology at George Washington University, is currently serving as President of the Society for the Scientific Study of Religion. Her book, *They Call Her Pastor*, was published in 1992.

Writing this book was a group effort, and the four authors share responsibility for the final product. Each author took primary responsibility for initial drafts of two or three chapters. Bill D'Antonio took the lead on chapters on human sexuality, the Church's most committed Catholics, Latinos, and the final chapter on future directions; Dean Hoge took the lead on the introductory chapter ("Whither American Catholicism?") and chapter two on moral authority. James Davidson had primary responsibility for chapters on three generations of Catholics and post-Vatican II Catholics, while Ruth Wallace was primarily responsible for the chapters on women's place in the Church and changes in parish life.

References

Abbott, Walter M. 1966. *The Documents of Vatican II.* Chicago: Herder and Herder.

Greeley, Andrew M. and William McManus. 1987. *Catholic Contributions: Sociology and Policy.* Chicago: The Thomas More Press.

Hoge, Dean R., Benton Johnson and Donald A. Luidens. 1994. *Vanishing Boundaries: The Religion of Mainline Protestant Baby Boomers.* Louisville: Westminster / John Knox Press.

1

Whither American Catholicism?

THAT THE CATHOLIC CHURCH IS NOT A DEMOCRACY IS NEWS TO NO ONE. Nor is it news to report that the Church through the pope and the bishops continues to defend traditional moral values. The real news is that despite the existence of very diverse and opposed positions on authority and moral teachings, our surveys of 1987 and 1993 show that the majority of American Catholics say they would never leave the Church. Rather, they are looking for ways to restructure it from within. Because, as they argue, "It's my Church too!" Meanwhile, Catholics on the right have emerged to defend traditional structures and teachings. This book maps the trends among these contending forces.

These challenges come at a time of rapid change in all areas of society, both nationally and internationally. And they raise questions about the directions the Catholic Church in America may take.

In this book we use sociological research to depict the laity's views on such issues as moral authority, human sexuality, the role of women, changes in parish structures, and commitment to the Church, and relate them to such variables as generational, gender and ethnic differences – comparing First Wave (European-origin) with Latino Catholics. These are the contested issues that have set laity against laity, and laity for and against the hierarchy. We analyze these issues over a thirty year time period, roughly since the end of Vatican II. Special attention is given to our 1987 and 1993 Gallup surveys, which permit us to provide a picture showing the trends of lay attitudes on governance and moral issues.

Our study clarifies how age and gender, education and ethnicity, and level of commitment affect the way laypersons see the Church. Despite the range and extent of disagreement, tension and conflict over issues as varied as the impact of the priest shortage on the survival of parishes, and access to the sacraments for divorced and remarried Catholics, surveys show that a great majority of American Catholics say they will never leave the Church (see especially Chapter 8). And a great majority of young Catholics still expect to bring their children up as Catholics (CFFC Survey, 1993). Our analysis provides an important step in trying to understand the forces that both divide and unite the Catholic laity as we approach a new millennium.

We begin our account with a review of the major themes in American Catholic history. Then we consider more recent developments, especially Vatican II and *Humanae Vitae*, and societal changes which have contributed to the laity's current attitudes, values and beliefs. This chapter ends with a paradigm which we find useful for assessing the laity's views of key issues facing the American Catholic Church today.

The Roots of American Catholicism: Two Waves of Immigration

At the time of the American Revolution only a few Catholics lived in the colonies, and most were in Maryland. Historians estimate the overall number at about 25,000 (Hennesey, 1981:73). The vast majority of Catholics arrived later, and they came in two major waves. The first wave began in about 1820 and grew more or less steadily until about 1910. The decades with the largest numbers of immigrants were 1900 to 1909, when 8.8 million immigrants arrived, and 1910 to 1919, when 5.7 million arrived. The majority of the newcomers were Catholics, especially after 1900. In 1830 there were only about 318,000 Catholics in the nation, but by 1920 there were an estimated 18 million (Dolan, 1985:255). Most of the immigrants were from Ireland, Germany, Italy, France, Poland and other Slavic countries. The vast majority settled in the economic core of the nation, roughly a rectangle with corners at Boston, Baltimore, Milwaukee, and St. Louis; the southern edge approximated the Potomac and Ohio Rivers. This remains the traditional heartland of American Catholicism.

The first wave was broken in 1925, when Congress severely restricted the numbers who could come. At that time many Americans were becoming alarmed at the multitude of non-English-speaking immigrants with possibly strange and dangerous political ideas, so they decided to close the doors. Whereas from 1910 to 1920 an average of 570,000 immigrants came each year, from 1925 to 1935 the average was only 160,000.

Immigration from 1924 to 1965 was at a low level (see Figure 1.1), but in 1965 Congress amended the McCarran-Walter Act to eliminate national quotas, which until then had greatly restricted non-European immigration. The gates to non-Europeans have been open

Figure 1.1
Legal Immigration to the United States by Decade

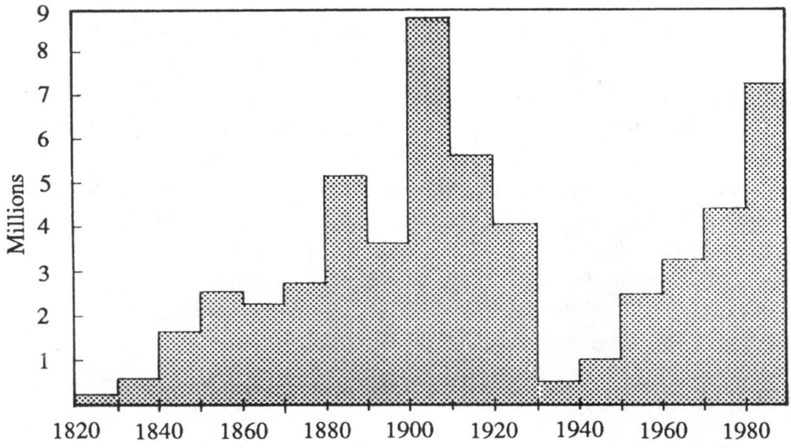

Source: *Historical Statistics of the U.S.A.* (1975) and recent U.S. census data.

ever since. Latinos have streamed in from Puerto Rico, Cuba, and Mexico, as well as from other Central and South American countries; Asians have migrated to the United States from Korea, Taiwan, mainland China, and Japan. This second wave of immigration is as large as the first and is destined to continue for a long time.

To what extent have the first-wave European immigrants assimilated into American society structurally and culturally? To what extent do they remain structurally and culturally separated? And, to what extent are the experiences of the second-wave immigrants likely to be the same or different?

The first wave of Catholic immigrants and their descendants have experienced considerable assimilation over the course of more than 150 years. Until well into this century they suffered prejudice and discrimination at all levels of society. Anti-Catholicism was institutionalized at the top of the society, where liberal Protestant groups, especially Episcopalians, Presbyterians, and Congregationalists (now the United Church of Christ) enjoyed disproportionate influence in virtually all spheres of American life (Davidson, 1994; Davidson, Pyle, & Reyes, forthcoming). It also pervaded the lower social classes, where groups such as the Know-Nothings and the Ku Klux Klan fought against the integration of blacks, Jews, and Catholics. Catholics responded by erecting barriers around themselves. They started their own schools, clubs, cooperatives, and lodges. Historians have called the prevailing attitude of Catholic leaders during this period a "siege mentality." The Vatican encouraged these reactions by its suspicion and condemnation of much that the United States represented, especially its *laissez faire* capitalism.[1]

Though structurally separated from American society, Catholics tended to assimilate culturally. Through organizations like Catholic Boy Scouts and Catholic schools for girls, Catholic organizations stressed the importance of becoming American and taking on American values. Catholics achieved socioeconomic parity with Protestants by the 1960s. The experiences of the Kennedy presidency, the papacy of John XXIII, and the Second Vatican Council decisively told American Catholics that they were fully American and that it was okay.

Meanwhile, Protestants' fear of Catholics subsided as increasing numbers of Catholics worked their way into the middle class. Non-Catholics felt reassured that Catholics could contribute to a democratic society. Though some structural barriers remained, European Catholics had culturally assimilated into the mainstream of American life.

What are the consequences of this assimilation? It has had, and is continuing to have, major consequences both within the Church and in the larger society. For example, the two pastoral letters on peace (1984) and the economy (1986) established the bishops as spokespersons on public issues. These were issues that extended well beyond the boundaries of the Catholic Church. In the case of the peace and economy pastorals, the bishops listened to critics from all sides, and modified their positions as a result. Their behavior reflected an appreciation for pluralism and compromise in public policy-making. Their letters won widespread admiration. However, in the 1990s, it has been argued (Burns, 1992) that their uncompromising stance against abortion may be undermining their recently-won legitimacy. As we will show in Chapter 3, a majority of American Catholics support the legality of abortion, and a significant minority believe it can be a moral choice under some circumstances. This fact has added to the complexity of the abortion issue in the public arena, making it increasingly problematic.

Assimilation is also proving problematic for the Church's teaching authority at the personal level, a major concern of this book. Fichter (1977:163-164) stated this viewpoint very well:

---

1. Again in this century, the popes have on several occasions been critical of the excesses of capitalism, for example, Paul VI's *Populorum Progressio* (1967), and John Paul II's *Laborem Exercens*. The American Catholic bishops must be credited with an effort to continue in this same vein with the pastoral letter on the Economy (1986), which letter was considerably softened after drafts were criticized by strong capitalist supporters Michael Novak and William Simon among others.

> The Church is being modernized in spite of itself. It appears that the changes are occurring at the bottom of the structure. . . . American Catholicism is experiencing adaptation at the grass roots. The most significant aspect of the change is the switch of emphasis in the basis of moral and religious guidance. Dependence on legislation from above has largely switched to dependence on the conscience of the people.

More recently, Kennedy (1984:158) has cogently stated the same argument:

> The essential changes of the coming decade will not follow from agreements or documents signed and sealed by church officials but from the already well-established attitudes and behavior of the believing community. . . . The best predictions about tomorrow are based on what people are doing today. These are the only reliable mega-trends.

As American Catholics of European backgrounds have embraced American culture, a second wave of Catholic immigrants has entered the picture. The second-wave group of most interest to us in this volume is the Latinos. Their importance derives from their numbers. Latinos will be the largest racial-ethnic minority in the United States within the next decade or two. Some 65 to 75 percent are reported to be Catholic, roughly 15 to 25 percent of the U.S. Catholic population.

To what extent will the experiences of the second wave of immigrants be similar to, or different from, those of the first-wave, European immigrants? There seem to be three possible answers. One emphasizes the similarities between first- and second-wave immigrants and contends that Latinos will assimilate much as the Europeans did. It stresses all immigrants' eagerness to improve their lot, their readiness to adapt to the "host society," the U.S. commitment to being the land of opportunity, and its readiness to absorb all who want a better life. Fitzpatrick (1971, 1987) has expressed this assimilationist view, as has Deck (1989), even as they have expressed concerns about its implications for certain features of Latino socioreligious life.

The second view emphasizes differences between first-and second-wave immigration and projects that Latinos will have a harder time assimilating. It contends that first-wave immigrants were white, they left their faraway homelands behind, and they entered a blue-collar society that offered them many opportunities for mobility in urban, industrial settings. Second-wave immigrants have known years of colonial rule in Mexico, Puerto Rico and Cuba; are more likely to suffer from racial and ethnic prejudice; are more able to perpetuate their cultural differences because of proximity to their homelands; and enter an increasingly white-collar, suburban-oriented society that doesn't provide them with as many lower-level opportunities as the first-wave immigrants had (Moore, 1976; Feagin & Feagin, 1993).

The third view is that second-wave immigrants will have an easier time assimilating because American society is more pluralistic and tolerant today than it was at the turn of the century (Connor, 1985:360; McLemore & Romo, 1985; Waters, 1990). According to this view, Americans are more highly educated and more open-minded than they used to be. Also, through experiences such as the civil rights movement, the nation has rejected its history of Anglocentrism and embraced a multi-cultural view of society. Thus, it is more ready now than ever before to accept and appreciate new ethno-religious traditions.

In our opinion, the future will be a struggle between the first scenario (the assimilationist view) and the second (the pluralist view). Second-wave immigrants will experience tremendous societal pressure to assimilate, and some of that pressure will come from the Church, which is now widely considered a "mainline religion" (Roof and McKinney, 1987). Latinos will be expected by societal leaders to fit into the American way of life and by church leaders to fit into an American Church. Yet the structural and cultural differences that distinguish second-wave immigrants from European immigrants are likely to make that assimilation difficult. Racial attitudes and economic conditions will continue to be barriers to full integration. The growing shortage of priests in general and Latino priests in particular will exacerbate the problem. And, despite church leaders' encouragement of the formation of faith communities (small Christian base communities) within Latino parishes to promote both spiritual growth and assimilation, the large size and organizational complexity of the Latino population and the ease of travel to and from nearby homelands will further complicate the process. There is also the question of how their own background and cultural traditions will affect their views on matters of governance and moral teachings, the main focus of this book. Chapter 9 provides a comparison of the views of First Wave and Latino Catholics on the main issues of our study. The third, and most optimistic, view seems least realistic of all.

Early Tensions between Americanists and Europeanists

The influx of European immigrants to the United States contributed to a rift between the Vatican and some leaders in American Catholicism. By the 1870s an "Americanist" faction was making itself heard in the United States. It advocated moving the Church in the direction of American values: separation of church and state, cooperation with other Christian denominations, autonomy from the Vatican, religious liberty under the law, and more democratic decision making in the Church (Greeley, 1967; Dolan, 1985). The Vatican was suspicious of such American tendencies and the attitudes of America's Protestant denominations (Hennesey, 1981:202).

Another factor exacerbated the problem. During the late nineteenth century, papal power in European political life diminished to the vanishing point. As that happened, the papacy turned its attention to life within the Church. The papacy, speaking as the magisterium, focused more and more attention on faith and moral issues (Burns, 1992). The magisterium sought to make its declarations binding on the consciences of individual Catholics. The consequences of that change have been increasingly problematic, especially in the issues of contraception and abortion right down to the present.

An important structural consequence was the emergence of clericalism in the United States. In place of earlier congregationalism and elected trustees having power in parishes (Dolan, 1985), church leaders asserted clerical power and took over dioceses and parishes in the name of top-down authority. By the end of the nineteenth century the shift was complete – from the earlier congregational-style parishes of the Revolutionary era to the hierarchical clergy-dominated parishes of 1900 (Dolan, 1985:192). Tension was inevitable between the advocates of the hierarchical church and the lovers of American individualism. Dolan (p. 222) outlined the Vatican mentality in the final decades of the nineteenth century:

> The United States prided itself on freedom and democracy, and new immigrants as well as longtime citizens cherished these qualities. Time and again, European priests bemoaned this "spirit of independence" prevalent among Americans, since such a spirit weakened the respect for authority deemed so necessary in the church. American culture encouraged such freedom and independence, especially in things religious; church authorities recognized this not only as a weakness of the culture, but as a threat to Catholicism as well.

The two factions, clearly visible by the 1880s, have been called the Americanists, or Americanizers, and the Europeanists, or anti-Americanizers (Greeley, 1967; Dolan, 1985; Holland, 1988). The Americanists wanted a Catholic Church independent of foreign interference, using English rather than Latin, and situated in a society granting religious freedom to all citizens. They believed in separation of church and state and in religious liberty for everyone. They favored cooperation with Protestants. They wanted a Church that could adapt to the current culture, and they wanted a Church active in forming and reforming the total society.

The Europeanists or anti-Americanizers, in contrast, believed in Vatican authority exemplified by the idea of papal infallibility, and clericalism. They desired a Church supported by the state without concern for religious liberty of citizens because they held to an institutional model, saying that the Church was the one perfect society and possessor of truth. They had no interest in helping the Church adapt to American or any other society. They maintained that the Church is the basis of truth in the nation, and error has no rights. The Europeanists saw the Vatican as the one and only seat of moral authority.

When the controversy heated up, Pope Leo XIII issued a letter in 1899, *Testem Benevolentiae*, siding with the Europeanist party and censuring the Americanists. In 1907 Pope Pius X issued a stronger letter criticizing modernist thought, *Pascendi Dominici Gregis*. He demanded that all priests take an oath against modernist theology. This settled the issue at the institutional level. Clerical conservatism and Vatican power prevailed in the Church for the next sixty years – though the assimilation processes continued.

> Catholicism was now deemed clearly a religion of hierarchal authority, and people learned not only to pray, but also to obey. Being Catholic meant to submit to the authority of God as mediated through the Church – its Pope, bishops, and pastors. In such a culture, the rights of the individual conscience were deemphasized, as each person was conditioned to submit to the external authority of the Church. (Dolan, 1985:224)

Toward Integration

European immigration was greatly restricted in the 1920s, and American Catholics gradually improved their levels of education, affluence, and contact with other Americans. Old World languages gradually gave way to English in church and school. The second and third generations grew up. Pressures were building for change, and change came in the 1960s.

The sixties were the most pivotal decade in the history of American Catholicism. Five events came in rapid succession. First, in 1960 John F. Kennedy was elected as the first Catholic president, and his easy embrace of his Catholicism while moving in the highest social circles gave Catholics everywhere new confidence. Lingering feelings that Catholics were not fully American or were not fully welcome began to dwindle. Second, Pope John XXIII, who had been elected in 1958, called for *aggiornamento*. He made dramatic steps in reaching out to Protestants, Jews, and other persons of goodwill everywhere in the world, assuring everyone of Catholic openness and willingness to cooperate. John XXIII had a level of papal popularity unprecedented in U.S. history. Third, the Second Vatican Council, called by John XXIII and completed during the papacy of Paul VI, brought far-reaching innovations in doctrine and practices. Fourth, Paul VI issued his Encyclical *Humanae Vitae (On Human Life)* in 1968. The encyclical's efforts to give new emphasis to conjugal love and responsible parenthood were largely ignored. Instead, all attention was focused on the Pope's reaffirmation of the ban on contraceptive birth control, leading to a sudden crisis of authority and a threat to all the positive gains of the previous eight years (Fox, 1995: x). And fifth, the events of the sixties in the United States launched a cultural revolution. It began with the civil rights movement, and was followed in rapid, often overlapping succession by the antiwar movement, then the counterculture movement, the women's movement, and the sexual revolution. Demonstrations filled city streets from Washington, D.C. to San Francisco; ghettoes burned in summer riots; campuses erupted in ugly confrontations; and hippies roamed across the land. All institutions, not just the Catholic Church, were permanently affected.

Vatican II

In many ways the Vatican Council was the most important of the 1960s events for the Catholic Church (Greeley, 1976; Ebaugh, 1991). The Council documents were welcomed by many Americans with joy and relief, because they solved some of the lingering problems of being a Catholic in the United States. Most important, the Council reversed earlier Catholic teaching by affirming the separation of church and state and religious liberty for all. In one stroke a major sore point for American Catholics was removed. Also, the Council redefined the

Church as the "People of God" and advocated increased democratization of church structures, a more participative liturgy, use of the vernacular in worship, reduction of rules of abstinence, ecumenical goodwill with other Christians, an open door to biblical scholarship, and greater self-determination for men's and women's orders. The majority of American Catholics welcomed these moves; the decades-old standoff between Americanizers and Europeanizers, was over – or so it seemed. Signs of new optimism and goodwill appeared everywhere. The siege mentality of the early twentieth century was gone. Ever since, the dominant mood of Catholics has been to embrace American society with little reservation, to enter all universities, corporations, and associations without hesitation, and to feel like full participants in American life (Greeley, 1967). Unfortunately, some of the enthusiasm engendered by Vatican II was lost by the negative impact of *Humanae Vitae* (Greeley, 1976, 1979), and now some three decades later, these two momentous events of the 1960s continue to divide Catholics here and abroad.

Social Changes

Catholics increasingly lived side by side with Protestants and Jews in America's expanding suburbs. The percentage of Catholic young people attending college climbed steadily. While Catholic college population grew, the vast majority of Catholics attended non-Catholic colleges; in the late 1980s the estimate was 90 percent (Hoge, 1987:45). The Catholic colleges and universities moved in the direction of American higher education ideals. Catholics rose in education and income, and non-Catholics lost their fear of voting for a Catholic for president. Polls demonstrate the changes.

The percentage of all Americans who have graduated from college rose steadily after about 1970. Catholics started at a much lower level in 1952 but caught up with Protestants by the end of the sixties (see Figure 1.2).

The average family income of Protestants and Catholics, both in raw dollars and in constant 1960 dollars (that is, after removing the effects of inflation) similarly moved upward, that of Catholic families slightly more (see Figure 1.3). An analysis of a 1992 Gallup poll states:

> Proportionately, Catholics nowadays are just as likely as Protestants to have attended and graduated from college, and even slightly more likely to enjoy above-average income. For example, Catholics represent 26 percent of the overall

Figure 1.2
Percent College Graduates in Population 18 and Over

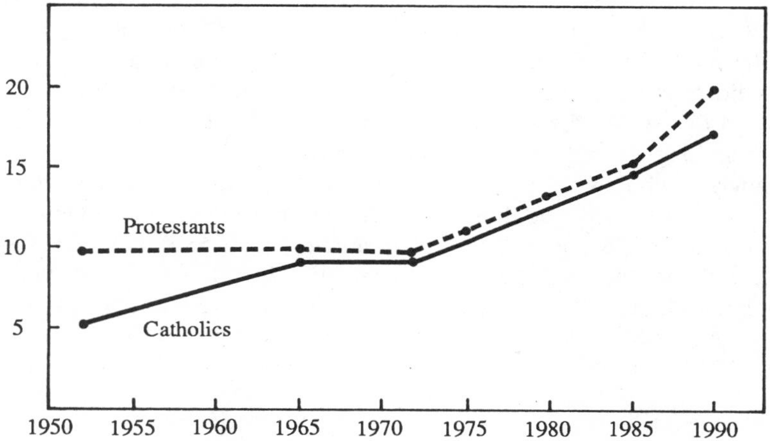

Source: Marty, Rosenberg, and Greeley (1968), p. 301; General Social Survey, 1972-90.

Figure 1.3
Mean Family Income

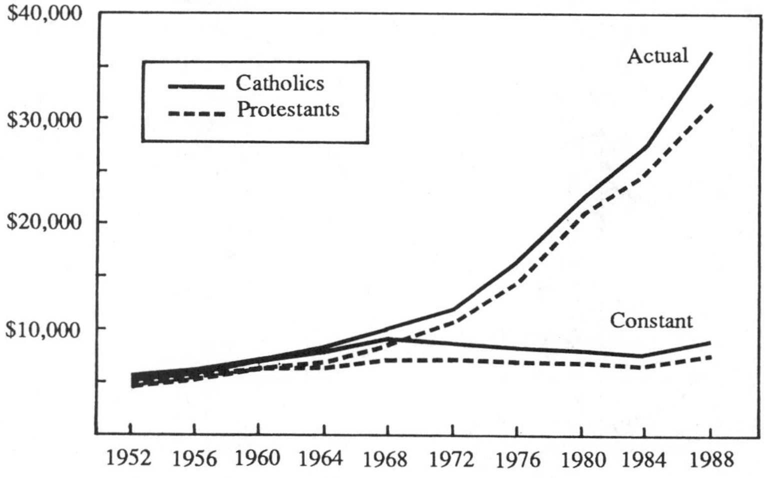

Source: American National Election Studies (Ann Arbor, Michigan).

population, but 30 percent of those with incomes of $75,000 or more. (*Emerging Trends*, 1993:5).

The assimilation of Catholics into all of society went on (see Figure 1.4). For instance, the percentage of American Protestants telling pollsters that they would be willing to vote for a Catholic presidential candidate jumped a dramatic 23 points from 1952 to 1965, then continued to rise. By the 1990s the question had lost its importance and was no longer being asked. Whether a candidate is Catholic no longer matters; Catholics are now full participants in politics. Another series of polls asked, "Do you think the Catholics are trying to get too much power in the U.S., or not?" In 1952, among American Protestants, 41 percent said yes; in 1965, 30 percent; in 1974, 11 percent. (*Gallup Opinion Index*, 1979:129). Anti-Catholic feelings were disappearing.

As Catholics converged with other Americans in values, their family-life patterns changed. The traditional large Catholic family soon

Figure 1.4
Percent of American Protestants
Who Would Vote for a Catholic for President

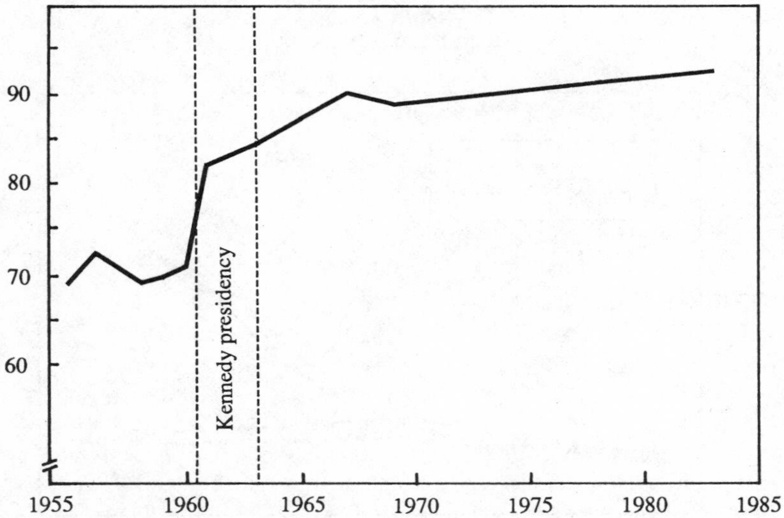

Source: Niemi, Mueller, and Smith (1989), p. 27.

disappeared as Catholic birth rates dropped to the level of Protestants by 1970 (Westoff, 1979:237). Child-rearing philosophies also changed to converge with Protestant views. In a classic trend study, Duane Alwin found that Catholics rearing children in the 1950s stressed obedience more and autonomy less than Protestants, but by the 1970s the Catholics' parental attitudes were the same as those of the Protestants. Rising levels of education were seen as a major reason (Alwin, 1986).

Catholics also participated in four cultural trends which were occurring throughout American society. First, Americans support civil liberties such as freedom of speech and freedom of expression today more than ever. For example, polls over time have asked Americans about "people whose ideas are considered bad or dangerous by other people." Should a person who "wanted to make a speech in your community against churches and religion" be allowed to speak? In 1952, 60 percent said no; in 1973, 34 percent; and in 1985, 34 percent again said no. And should an admitted communist be allowed to make a speech in one's community? In 1952, 68 percent said no; in 1972, 46 percent, and in 1985, 41 percent. (*Public Opinion,* July/August 1987: 29). Researchers who monitor anti-Semitism have seen a steady decrease in the past half century. Tom W. Smith of the National Opinion Research Center said that anti-Semitism "decreased appreciably" after World War II as "Jews became more accepted in the mainstream of American life." For example, polls asked Americans to agree or disagree with the statement "Jews are more willing than others to use shady practices to get what they want." In 1964, 48 percent agreed, and in 1992, 22 percent. Thirty percent agreed with the statement "Jews don't care what happens to anyone but their own kind," in 1964, but only 16 percent in 1992 (*Washington Post*, 21 June 1994).

Second, a sexual revolution and a gender revolution got under way in the 1960s, each with lasting effects. Attitudes about premarital sex moved in the direction of individual prerogative. In a 1969 poll, 68 percent of Americans said they disapproved of premarital sex; by 1985 this had dropped to 39 percent (*Emerging Trends,* 1985). After the middle 1980s attitudes changed little. Approval of sex education in schools has grown from the 1960s onward. Approval of making birth control information available to adults began rising in the 1960s and is almost unanimous today (Smith, 1990:418). Cohabitation of unmarried persons has increased. In all of the attitude areas regarding sexuality the greatest changes occurred prior to the 1980s, and from that time until now the changes have been small (Smith, 1990).

Third, family life changed considerably. The most dramatic aspect was the entry of millions of women into the work force. Attitudes on family size changed. A series of polls have asked Americans about the ideal number of children, and the responses have moved dramatically since the mid-1960s toward smaller families (see Figure 1.5).

Figure 1.5
Percentage of Americans:
Ideal Number of Children in a Family is Three or More

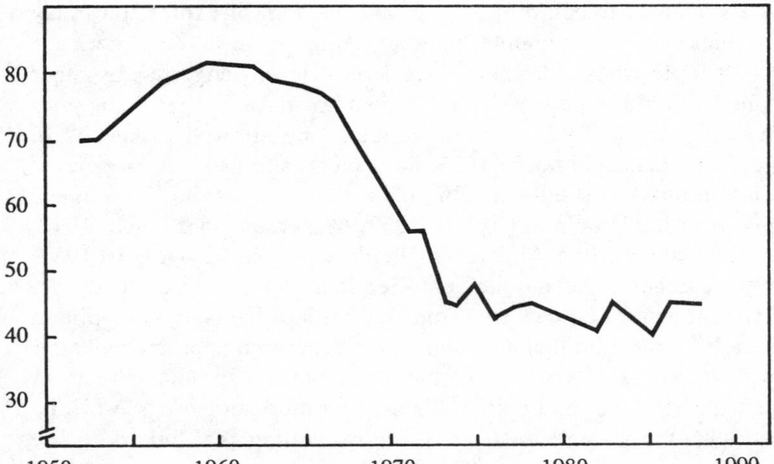

Source: Niemi, Mueller, and Smith (1989), p. 269.

Further, Americans have become more accepting of interfaith marriage. Several polls asked, "Do you approve or disapprove of marriage between Catholics and Protestants?" In 1968, 63 percent of Americans approved; in 1978, 72 percent; and in 1983, 79 percent (*Emerging Trends,* 1983:5).

Finally, there also has been a trend – especially among Americans with the most schooling – away from traditional religion toward greater humanism (Marsden and Longfield, 1992; Hoge, Johnson, and Luidens, 1994). Traditional religion's emphasis on other-worldliness and absolute truth has been severely challenged by humanism's emphasis on this-worldly concerns and the relativity of truth. A 1991 Gallup poll, asked, "What is the most believable authority in matters of truth? Is it personal experience, Scripture, parents, science, the media, or religious leaders?" Thirty-seven percent of adults with less than a high school education picked Scripture, compared to only 23 percent of college graduates, who gave more authority to personal experience and science (*Emerging Trends*, 1992:4). Some say this shift has contributed to the decline of the Protestant mainline.

Toward Restoration

Vatican II brought a sudden opening for institutional change. It was as if a floodgate across a river had been raised. Change came pell-mell. Liturgical experiments were carried out, statues were removed from churches, religious orders and seminaries made far-reaching innovations, and new forms of local governance were developed. Taken as a whole, the changes were in the direction of mainstream American culture. The trappings of Catholicism that looked Old World or bizarre from that angle were trimmed back. Pressures had been building for two decades, and now all at once changes could be realized. The model of a river and a floodgate is useful because it distinguishes underlying pressures from the gatekeeping power of institutional decisions (Hoge, 1986). Berger (1992:44) comments:

> Until [the Council] the Catholic church in America had successfully maintained a robust subculture whose inhabitants were kept relatively safe from the surrounding cognitive turbulence. Vatican II intended, in the words of John XXIII, to "open windows in the wall"; the unintended consequence of this so-called *aggiornamento* was to open an eight-lane superhighway through the center of the Catholic ghetto – everything came roaring in. The present leadership of the Catholic church, especially the Rome headquarters, is trying hard to repair the fortifications; chances are that it is too late, at least in Western countries.

By the 1980s and 1990s the institutional floodgates were being lowered again by Pope John Paul II. He changed the personnel in charge of appointing bishops, so that more appointments were of conservatives. He declared the issues of birth control, priestly celibacy, and women's ordination to be closed to discussion. He began monitoring theological seminaries to curb the influence of women teachers and to avoid a leveling of clergy and laity. He censured an archbishop in Seattle and dismissed a theology professor at the Catholic University of America who leaned in the direction of lay participation and freedom of conscience. He issued directives setting guidelines for the teaching of

Catholic theology in universities. He forced professors of theology to take oaths of fidelity to the teaching of the magisterium. His encyclical *Veritatis Splendor* called for a renewed emphasis on traditional moral virtues.

The pope is not alone in his efforts to restore traditional norms and values. Cardinal Ratzinger, many of the pope's recently appointed bishops, Mother Angelica, Opus Dei, and Catholics United for the Faith also are leaders (see Dinges and Hitchcock, 1991 for a more complete analysis). There are other signs that many Catholic lay people agree with the pope's affirmation of traditional teachings. Millions of Catholic lay persons have flocked to the pope's recent pilgrimages to places such as the United States and the Philippines. The Church's new catechism and the pope's book, *Crossing the Threshold of Hope,* are selling well worldwide. A recent study showed that a majority of Catholics in Indiana approve of the pope's leadership and want the Church to put more emphasis on tradition (Davidson, 1995).

There also were increasing signs of resistance to the cultural trends of the 1970s and 1980s. Significant voices criticized the changes during the 1980s, such as President Ronald Reagan's urging that Americans get "back to the basics." Efforts to restore traditional values have gained momentum in the 1990s. There have been more and more efforts to reverse the so-called "liberal agenda" and restore traditional "family values." Examples are the new Christian Right's grassroots effort to gain control of local governments and school boards; Dan Quayle's highly publicized objections to Murphy Brown's decision to be a single parent; and conservative Republicans' resounding victories in the 1994 election.

Significant numbers of Catholic laity support these recent efforts to reaffirm traditional moral and political values. Catholic Pat Buchanan was one of the most visible and vocal spokespersons for the conservative wing at the 1992 Republican convention. Many Catholics supported the conservative Republican candidates who in 1994 became the majority in the U.S. House of Representatives for the first time in over 40 years.

By the mid-1990s, then, tensions were so high that, in some ways at least, Hunter's (1991) concept of "culture wars" seemed an apt description of the societal conflict between liberals and conservatives, between integrationists and restorationists. Within the American Catholic Church, historic tensions between those who want full integration into American society and those who want to restore traditional church teachings and decision-making processes took on new meaning.

Whither American Catholicism? A Political Perspective

As we wonder about future directions in the Church, we find it useful to look through a political lens. This approach emphasizes the fact that diverse groups vie with one another to see that church policies and practices reflect their competing values and interests. Groups with different priorities and preferences try to affect the decisions religious leaders make at key "choice points" (Winter, 1977). The groups which prevail at these choice points will chart the future course of the Catholic Church in America.[2]

Competing Groups

Today's Church is comprised of Catholics who differ by age, levels of education, gender, region of the country, and race/ethnicity. Our study examines aspects of these dimensions within American Catholicism.

Stature in the Church, as elsewhere in society, tends to be distributed unequally along racial, ethnic, gender, and age lines. Whites, European ethnics, men, and older persons have had the best access to the most important roles in the Church. Blacks, Latinos/as, women, and young persons have tended to be marginalized. We devote separate chapters to these groups, exploring the extent to which they tend toward the integrationist perspective or the restorationist view of the Church.

Among lay people, ability to participate in decision-making in church affairs has been very limited. Even Catholics for whom the issues have high salience and who participate most actively in their parishes and dioceses have had little influence on church teachings affecting their lives. Thus, we examine the different ways more and less committed lay people think about a wide variety of issues involving participation in church decision-making. And we will show how the laity expresses its personal power by the way it reacts to a range of church teachings on moral issues.

Specific Choice Points

What are some of these issues? Which choice points are likely to have the greatest impact on future directions in the Church? Some of the more prominent ones concern membership, authority, belief,

---

2. We share this perspective with many others who study organizations in general (e.g. Perrow, 1986; Bolman and Deal, 1991, sociologists of religion who investigate religious organizations (e.g., Wood, 1981; Davidson and Koch, 1995), and colleagues who look specifically at the Catholic Church (e.g., Seidler and Meyer, 1989; Burns, 1992).

practice and societal relationships (see Table 1.1). Each of these issues encompasses many interrelated concerns and offers a wide variety of options.

Table 1.1
Dimensions of the Integrationist-Restorationist Continuum

	Integrationist Choices	*Restorationist Choices*
Membership		
Criteria	Inclusive	Exclusive
Commitment	Voluntary	Obligatory
Authority		
Decision-Making	Democratic	Hierarchical
Leadership	Lay-led	Clergy-led
Access to authority	Open to all	Limited to males
Belief and practice		
Theological norm	Pluralism	Uniformity
Faith and morals	Relative	Absolute
Cultural norm	Multi-cultural	European
Emphasis	Innovation	Tradition
Societal Relations		
Relationship with host society	Culture affirming	Counter-cultural
Relationship with other religions	Ecumenical	Parochial

Leaders debate membership issues such as the inclusivity or exclusivity of belonging to the Church, and the extent to which membership is a matter of individual choice or historical and ancestral obligation. Is the Church for all who profess belief in Christ, or is it only for those who embrace specifically-Catholic teachings such as papal infallibility? To what extent should the Church be a voluntary association comprised of people who make personal decisions for Christ? To what extent is membership tied to one's ethnic and family ancestry? To what extent does being Catholic require accountability to tradition and/or imply individual freedom to work out one's beliefs and practices through reason and experience?

Clergy and lay leaders also have expressed differing views on a variety of authority-related issues such as the nature of decision making, leadership, access to authority, and communication. To what extent should decision-making be concentrated at the top of a hierarchical institution or more widely distributed? To what extent should leadership be limited to clergy or shared with lay people? Who should have access to authority: males only or all persons regardless of gender? What form should communication take: top-down communiqués from the hierarchy to the laity, or dialogue leading to a consensus among all parties? On changes in parish life (Chapter 7), for example, we show that the vast majority of laity want the right to participate in decisions ranging from use of parish income to selection of parish priests.

Other choice points concern the Church's orientations toward belief and practice. To what extent should the Church review its moral teachings in the light of new biblical scholarship, historical work and theological insights? To what extent should the Church affirm the validity of theological pluralism? How much should it encourage experimentation with new ideas and innovative forms of ministry? Conversely, to what extent should the Church emphasize compliance with the Church's Roman (European) theological traditions?

These concerns are expressed in decisions regarding "faith and morals." Other research (Ryba, 1994; Davidson, 1995) has shown that among lay people there are high levels of consensus on core faith issues such as the Trinity, Incarnation, the Virgin Birth, the Resurrection, and Transubstantiation (belief that at Mass the bread and wine are transformed into the Body and Blood of Christ). Clergy and laity alike affirm the centrality of these doctrines. They are not contested issues.

There is more disagreement on moral teachings. Clergy and lay people express a wide range of views on issues such as abortion, divorce and remarriage, birth control, and pre-marital sex. The trends show women (Chapter 6) in growing disagreement with the traditional teachings. These are the hotly contested issues – the focal points of political tension in the Church today. The decisions church leaders make on these issues will have enormous impact on future directions in the Church.

Another set of issues concerns the Church's relationships with its social and religious environment. How open should the Church be to competing ideas and groups? To what extent should it embrace American values and tolerate religious groups with different beliefs and practices? How much should the Church stand "over against" the prevailing culture and religious groups which foster opposing worldviews? How ecumenical should the Church be?

General Orientations

In the 19th century, the Church was torn between "Americanists" who wanted the Church to assimilate into American society and "Europeanists" who wanted to preserve the Church's traditional teachings and structures (Greeley, 1967; Dolan, 1985; Holland,1988). Americanists such as Bishop Ireland of Minnesota wanted to embrace American culture and all the changes it might imply for the Church, including individual freedom and more democratic decision making. Europeanists – "mainly . . . French-born clerics and German-born priests and lay people" (Dolan, 1985:294) – stressed the importance of protecting the Church's teachings and hierarchical structures against the evils of American culture.

One hundred and twenty-five years after Vatican I (1870) and 30 years after Vatican II (1962-65), the options are quite similar, though certainly not identical. The Church can choose an "integrationist" course or it can pursue a "restorationist" approach (Holland, 1988). Describing the options in such polar terms oversimplifies real complexities, but it calls our attention to a fundamental polarity which cuts across many specific debates.

Reading down the two columns in Table 1.1, we see that restorationism today stresses exclusive membership and accountability; emphasizes that authority should be lodged in hierarchical positions occupied by male clergy with decisions being handed down to laity in one-way communications; stresses the need for compliance with Roman traditions and absolute truths, especially the Church's moral teachings based on natural law; feels the Church has gone too far in affirming American culture; and wants to restore the Church's emphasis on truth and the need to speak prophetically against heretical voices.

Integrationism puts more emphasis on inclusive membership and voluntary commitment; feels authority should be shared by clergy and laity so church decisions reflect all "the people of God," not just the hierarchy; hopes for fuller appreciation of the way faith and morals are shaped by specific contexts and consequences; advocates experimentation with new forms of ministry; affirms the prevailing culture; and cooperates with other religious groups.

The banners of restoration and integration are carried by very high profile groups. Pope John Paul II, Cardinal Ratzinger, Richard John Neuhaus, and Catholics United for the Faith advocate restorationist views on most of the issues in Table 1.1. Proponents of integrationism especially regarding the mode of decision-making include Joan Chittister, Rosemary Radford Ruether, Anthony Padovano, Charles

Curran, Richard McBrien and members of Call to Action. These conflicting parties struggle for control over the Church's future in America.

The vast majority of Catholic clergy and laity fall somewhere between the most extreme expressions of this debate. While a few are radical integrationists and some are radical restorationists, most Catholics have views which reflect a combination of both dispositions. Some Catholics prefer an integrationist approach, but feel a need to restore some traditional emphases. Others want to restore tradition, but acknowledge the need to affirm at least some elements of American society.

One of our goals is to learn how integrationist-oriented and restorationist-oriented American Catholics tend to be. Are they as integrationist as they were in the mid-1960s (Greeley, 1967)? Or have they moved closer to one or the other end of the integrationist-restorationist continuum? Have their orientations remained stable since our 1987 survey (D'Antonio, Davidson, Hoge and Wallace, 1989), or have they moved in one direction or the other? Are American Catholics more integration-oriented now than they were in the late 1980s? Or, are they more restoration-oriented? After we examine these trends in specific chapters, we will draw some overall conclusions in our final chapter.

Conclusions

Today's Church inherits a history of European immigration and considerable assimilation into American society. It also is experiencing a second wave of Latin American immigration. Whether this wave will duplicate the assimilation of the earlier wave or have a more pluralistic experience remains to be seen. The Church also is living in the wake of Vatican II and *Humanae Vitae*, which precipitated the most sweeping changes the Church had seen in over one hundred years. It also has been affected by societal and cultural shifts in the direction of individualism and cultural relativism.

There are increasing voices of discontent. In the Church a number of clergy and laity are asking for a return to traditional beliefs and practices. In society more generally, increasingly vigorous efforts are being made to reverse recent trends toward humanism (Carter, 1993).

All of these forces are at work as Catholics grapple with decisions which will affect the American Church's future well into the next century. We focus special attention on the laity's role in transforming the American Catholic Church. More specifically, we highlight the role that different groups of lay people are likely to play as they try to influence decisions church leaders will make in areas such as membership, authority, belief and practice, and societal relations. Now we turn to the specific groups, contested issues, and general orientations that form the backbone of our analysis. We begin with an analysis of the laity's views on authority.

References

Alwin, Duane F. 1986. "Religion and Parental Child-Rearing Orientations: Evidence of a Catholic-Protestant Convergence." *American Journal of Sociology* 92 (September): 412-440.

Berger, Peter L. 1992. *A Far Glory: The Quest for Faith in an Age of Credulity.* Garden City, NY: Doubleday.

Bolman, Lee G. and Terrence E. Deal. 1991. *Reframing Organizations: Artistry, Choice, and Leadership.* San Francisco: Jossey-Bass.

Burns, Gene. 1992. *The Frontiers of Catholicism: The Politics of Ideology in a Liberal World.* Berkeley: University of California Press.

Carter, Stephen. 1993. *The Culture of Disbelief.* New York: Basic Books.

Connor, Walker. 1985. *Mexican Americans in Comparative Perspective.* Washington, D.C.: Urban Institute.

D'Antonio, William V., James D. Davidson, Dean Hoge, and Ruth Wallace. 1989. *American Catholic Laity in a Changing Church.* Kansas City: Sheed & Ward.

Davidson, James D. 1994. "Religion Among America's Elite: Persistence and Change in the Protestant Establishment," *Sociology of Religion* (December): 419-440.

________. 1995. "Identity and the Various Subcultures Found within the Church Today" paper presented at Symposium on Culture and Catholic Identity, Orlando, FL.: Florida Catholic Conference, January.

________, and Jerome R. Koch. 1994. "Beyond Mutual and Public Benefits: The Inward and Outward Orientations of Non-Profit Organizations," Working Paper 202, Project on Non-Profit Organizations. New Haven, CT.: Yale University.

________, Ralph Pyle, and David Reyes. Forthcoming. "Persistence and Change in the Protestant Establishment, 1930-1992," *Social Forces.*

Deck, Allan Figueroa, S.J. 1989. *The Second Wave: Hispanic Ministry and the Evangelization of Cultures.* New York: Paulist Press.

Dinges, William D. and James Hitchcock. 1991. "Roman Catholic Traditionalism and Activist Conservatism in the United States," In Martin E. Marty and R. Scott Appleby (eds.), *Fundamentalisms Observed.* Chicago: University of Chicago Press. pp. 66-141.

Dolan, Jay P. 1985. *The American Catholic Experience.* Garden City, NY: Doubleday.

Ebaugh, Helen Rose (ed.) 1991. *Vatican II and U.S. Catholicism.* Greenwich, CT.: JAI Press.

Emerging Trends (Princeton Religious Research Center). 1985. "Majority Now Considers Premarital Sex Acceptable." Vol. 7(May): 3.

________. 1992. "What Is Truth?" Vol. 14 (February): 1, 4.

________. 1993. "Catholics Are Becoming the New Middle Class." Vol. 15 (March): 5.

Feagin, Joe R., and Clarice Booher Feagin. 1993. *Racial and Ethnic Relations.* Englewood Cliffs, NJ: Prentice-Hall.

Fichter, Joseph H. 1977. "Restructuring Catholicism." *Sociological Analysis* 38, no. 2: 154-164.

Fitzpatrick, Joseph. 1971. *Puerto Rican Americans.* Englewood Cliffs, NJ: Prentice-Hall.

________. 1987. *One Church, Many Cultures.* Kansas City, MO: Sheed & Ward.

Fox, Thomas C. 1995. *Sexuality and Catholicism.* New York: George Braziller.

Gallup Opinion Index. 1979. Report 169.

Gordon, Milton M. 1978. *Human Nature, Class, and Ethnicity.* New York: Oxford University Press.

Greeley, Andrew M. 1967. *The Catholic Experience.* New York: Doubleday and Co.

________. 1976. *Catholic Schools in a Declining Church.* Kansas City, MO: Andrews & McMeel.

________. 1979. *Crisis in the Church.* Chicago: The Thomas More Association.

Hennesey, James, S.J. 1981. *American Catholics.* New York: Oxford University Press.

Hoge, Dean R. 1986. "Interpreting Change in American Catholicism: The River and the Floodgate." *Review of Religious Research* 27:4 (June): 289-92.

________. 1987. *The Future of Catholic Leadership.* Kansas City, MO: Sheed & Ward.

________, Benton Johnson, and Donald A. Luidens. 1994. *Vanishing Boundaries: The Religion of Mainline Protestant Baby Boomers.* Louisville: Westminster/John Knox Press.

Holland, Joe. 1988. "Faith and Culture: An Historic Moment for the American Catholic Laity?" In Joe Holland and Anne Barsanti, (eds.), *American and Catholic: The New Debate*, South Orange, NJ: Pillar Books: 20-42.

Hunter, James Davison. 1991. *Culture Wars.* New York: Basic Books.

Kennedy, Eugene. 1984. *The Now and Future Church: The Psychology of Being an American Catholic.* Garden City, NY: Doubleday.

Kurtz, Lester R. 1986. *The Politics of Heresy: The Modernist Crisis in Roman Catholicism.* Berkeley: University of California Press.

Marsden, George M., and Bradley J. Longfield, 1992. *The Secularization of the Academy.* New York: Oxford University Press.

McLemore, S. Dale, and Ricardo Romo. 1985. "The Origins and Development of the Mexican American People" In McLemore and Romo, (eds.), *The Mexican American Experience.* Austin: University of Texas Press.

Moore, Joan. 1976. *Mexican Americans*. Englewood Cliffs, NJ: Prentice-Hall.

Neuhaus, Richard John. 1987. *The Catholic Moment: The Paradox of the Church in the Postmodern World*. San Francisco: Harper & Row.

Parrillo, Vincent N. 1985. *Strangers to These Shores: Race and Ethnic Relations in the United States*. 2nd ed. New York: Macmillan.

Perrow, Charles, 1986. *Complex Organizations: A Critical Essay*. 3rd Edition. New York: Random House.

Public Opinion. 1987. "The State of Intolerance in America." Vol. 10:2 July/August: 21-31.

Roof, Wade Clark, and William McKinney. 1987. *American Mainline Religion: Its Changing Shape and Future*. New Brunswick, NJ: Rutgers University Press.

Ryba, Thomas. 1994. "Theological Orientations: Pre-Vatican II and Post-Vatican II Beliefs," paper presented at the annual meeting of the Religious Research Association, Albuquerque, NM: November.

Schoenherr, Richard A., and Lawrence A. Young. 1993. *Full Pews and Empty Altars*. Madison: University of Wisconsin Press.

Seidler, John and Katherine Meyer. 1989. *Conflict and Change in the Catholic Church*. New Brunswick, N.J.: Rutgers University Press.

Smith, Tom W. 1990. "The Polls – A Report: The Sexual Revolution?" *Public Opinion Quarterly* 54:3 (Fall): 415-435.

Washington Post. 1994. "Study Cites Drop in Antisemitism." June 21: 19.

Waters, Mary C. 1990. *Ethnic Options: Choosing Identities in America*. Berkeley: University of California Press.

Weber, Max. 1964. *The Theory of Social and Economic Organization*. New York: The Free Press.

Westoff, Charles F. 1979. "The Blending of Catholic Reproductive Behavior." In Robert Wuthnow, (ed.), *The Religious Dimension*. New York: Academic Press: 231-240.

Winter, J. Alan. 1977. *Continuities in the Sociology of Religion*. New York: Harper and Row.

Wood, James R. 1981. *Leadership in Voluntary Organizations*. New Brunswick, N.J.: Rutgers University Press.

2

Maintaining Church Moral Authority

CHURCH AUTHORITY IS PROBABLY THE MOST CENTRAL ISSUE FACING American Catholicism. The Church has always claimed authority for its teachings on morality. In the early years the apostles asserted authority from their own first-hand experiences with Christ or from the recorded teachings of Christ. As centuries passed, the Church based authority for its moral teaching on the New Testament canon, on apostolic succession, and on the sanctity of age-old Christian tradition. Today all indications are that the Catholic Church's doctrinal and moral authority is diminishing. Observers say that it is weaker now than several decades ago. What has been lost? Why? To understand, we need to take a look at the nature of authority in general and how it rises or falls.

Measuring Authority

The most-quoted sociological definition of authority is Max Weber's: "the probability that certain specific commands from a given source will be obeyed by a given group of persons" (1947:324). *Authority* refers specifically to voluntary obedience, in contrast to *coercion*, which connotes non-voluntary obedience. If people obey a leader's commands voluntarily and not merely because of force or the threat of force, they do so because they recognize the leader's authority, and in that situation the leader's commands are "legitimate."

Authority entails not merely a proclamation by a leader but also the probability that a follower or group of followers will accept the proclamation and obey it. That is, authority has two elements, *claimed* authority and *accepted* authority. The former is the claim of the would-be leader and the latter is the empirical level of acceptance of the claim by followers. Whether a claim to authority is accepted or not is entirely in the hands of the followers, who make their own decisions based on their perceptions of the leader, the office held by the leader, and the leader's justification for the claim. We need to be clear that this analysis does not pertain to situations in which commands given are backed up by force or the threat of force. For example, a conquering army may take over a province and its leader issue decrees for the population to obey. The people will do so only because they fear for their lives.

The case of naked force backing a command does not occur in religious life in modern Western nations. Religious teachings in these nations must ask for voluntary acceptance from the followers. The followers will obey the teachings if they believe that the teachings are legitimate, justified, and true to the will of God. If they doubt the claims from which the teachings arise, they will follow their own wills or obey other teachings that they find more persuasive.

Claimed authority and accepted authority must not be confused. Normally there is a gap between them; more authority is claimed than accepted. To estimate the gap a researcher needs to measure, insofar as possible, both entities – claimed authority and accepted authority. Claimed authority can be measured, at least approximately, by studying the bases of moral claims, normally found in religious texts or church documents. This is usually the work of theologians and philosophers. To measure accepted authority is a different kind of task. It requires empirical measures of the degree to which followers accept the teachings or commands.

Claims for authority may be either institutional or personal. A leader may demand obedience based on his or her office or on personality or charisma. Catholic leaders normally depend on the authority of office and remind the faithful of the institution's history, traditions, and legitimacy. When that is sufficient to induce obedience, their authority is strong, predictable, and stable. But if the followers lose faith in the institution, any authority based on church office is shaky. Then leaders need to make appeals on the basis of their personal moral authority, personal charisma, and the strength of whatever arguments they can muster.

Claimed authority also varies in scope. A teacher may claim a wide or a narrow domain. Similarly, the follower has conceptions of how broad the leader's authority really is. This is the source of the frequent statement "I wish those priests would stay out of politics and stick to religious things that they know something about."

How firm is the Church's accepted authority today? Most observers think that it has weakened since the 1960s. Andrew Greeley has argued again and again that the Vatican's 1968 encyclical on reproduction, *Humanae Vitae*, created a crisis in credibility and authority that has never been resolved. Greeley believes that it has had far-reaching consequences in that it caused millions of Catholic laity to question if the pope's words are really authoritative and if people can have total faith that the pope is speaking the mind of God (Greeley *et al*, 1976: Chapter 5; Greeley, 1990:90-91). Other observers have agreed with him (see Dolan, 1987; Bianchi and Ruether, 1992).

We have good reason to believe that the Church's moral authority has weakened since the 1960s, especially in the areas of sexual morality. Evidence for this is that the vast majority of Catholics today use some form of birth control, which *Humanae Vitae* disallows. All during the 1970s, 1980s, and 1990s, research studies showed a widening gap between Church teachings and lay attitudes on birth control, divorce, and related topics. For example, in a 1967 survey, 41 percent of adult Catholics favored the use of birth control devices, and 27 percent said that they had used such devices in their own family (*Newsweek*, 1967:71-72). In 1963 over half of American Catholics accepted the Church's teaching that birth control was wrong; in a 1987 poll only 18 percent said it was.[1] A 1993 survey found only 13 percent of Catholics holding that conviction. In the same survey, only 12 percent of Catholics under age 50 said they agreed with "all" church teachings on faith and morality; of those 50 and older, the figure was 28 percent.[2] The act of disobeying a church pronouncement, especially when a person knows that millions of others are also doing it, creates alienation from the pronouncement itself.

The problem is general, not limited to specific teachings. Since the middle of the nineteenth century the Catholic Church in the United States has been in tension with the democratic, individualistic American culture. As Catholics assimilated to the culture, tensions rose. Like all educated Americans, from the 1960s on, Catholics began examining the authority claims of institutions more closely than ever. They began insisting that constituents must be involved in the decision making of

---

1. "Research Report on August 14-19, 1987 Nationwide Poll #128," duplicated copy from *Los Angeles Times*.

2. "How U.S. Catholics View Their Church," *USA Today*, 10 August 1993, p. 6A. Based on a *USA Today*/CNN/Gallup poll. Numerous polls of Catholics were done in 1993 on the occasion of the pope's visit. A 1993 poll of Catholics in Canada, published in *McLean's*, 12 April 1993, found that artificial birth control was approved by 91 percent; 84 percent would allow priests to marry; 78 percent favored allowing women to become priests; and 55 percent said that homosexual behavior is morally acceptable. These figures are higher than in the United States.

any institution that deserves authority. Claims by the pope that his pronouncements carried authority because of apostolic succession met with more and more skepticism. And let us remember that this kind of institutional claim is in tension with the American temper and the very thing the U.S. Constitution was written to restrict. After the Second Vatican Council, Catholics were unclear about how legitimate the pope's claims to moral authority really were and about how much authority people should accord to the voice of conscience. A *Newsweek* (1967:75) article stated the issue:

> No issue divides conservative and liberal Catholics more than the question of where church authority ends and individual freedom begins. "The Pope keeps talking about the teaching authority, or magisterium, of the church," says New York's Father Francis X. Murphy, professor of church history at the College of St. Alphonsus in Rome, "but he doesn't define what that authority is. This is precisely the problem bedeviling theologians today."

A series of polls have asked American Catholics to agree or disagree with this statement: "Jesus directly handed over the leadership of His Church to Peter and the Popes." In 1963, 86 percent said the statement was certainly or probably true; in 1974, 71 percent; and in 1985, 68 percent (Hoge, 1987:57), a decline of 18 points in a span of twenty-two years.

Other events besides Vatican II caused change. The political and cultural turmoil in the United States in the 1960s undoubtedly had an effect. The powerful experiences of those years heightened mistrust of *all* institutions among many Americans, especially the young. When the lies and dissembling of national leaders and even presidents were revealed during the Vietnam era, when the duplicity of President Nixon came to light in the Watergate scandal, and when a president and other beloved national figures were assassinated, skepticism about government rose to new heights. People concluded that the whole system was rotten,[3] and faith in government has not returned to its pre-1970 level (see Figure 2.1).

In sixteen surveys since the early 1950s, the National Election Study asked voting-age adults whether they agreed or disagreed with this statement: "I don't think that public officials care much what people like me think." In 1952, 36 percent agreed; in the mid-to-late 1970s,

---

3. In a suburb of Washington, D.C., a number of cars carry bumper stickers saying "Question Authority," a slogan that seems to be an identity statement for one portion of the post-sixties youth culture.

Figure 2.1
Percentage of Americans:
Government Can Be Trusted All or Most of the Time

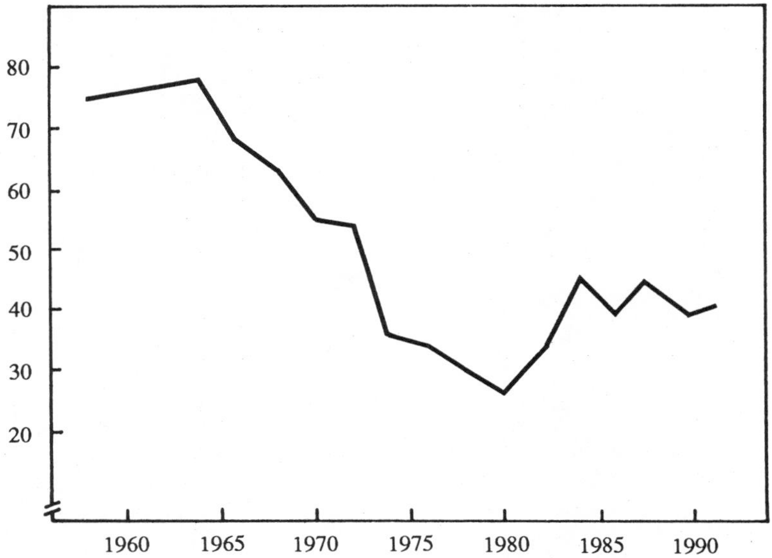

Source: *Washington Post,* November 3, 1991. Based on National Election Studies and *Washington Post-ABC News* Polls. 1987-88 are combined.

Q: "How much of the time do you trust the government in Washington to do what is right: just about always, most of the time, or only some of the time?"

about 54 percent; in 1991, 59 percent. The 1964 National Election Study found that 31 percent of Americans said government was run by a "few big interests"; in 1991, 71 percent expressed that view (Balz and Morin, 1991).

Skepticism toward large institutions since the early 1970s has infected organized religion as well, although indications are that the impact was milder. Evidence is scanty, but we do possess nationwide polls on public confidence in various institutions, including organized religion (see Figure 2.2 for trends since the relevant questions were first asked in 1966).

Figure 2.2
Percentage of Americans Having a "Great Deal of Confidence" in the People in Charge of Running Organized Religion

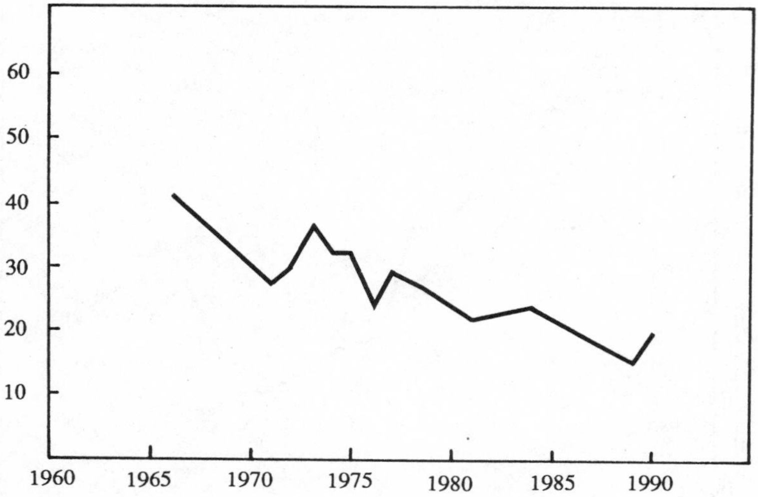

Source: Harris Polls. *Public Opinion*, Oct./Nov. 1979, p. 30; *Emerging Trends,* January 1991, p. 6; *Public Opinion Quarterly,* 40:4, p. 545. 1978-1979 are combined.

The downward slide in confidence in organized religion is much more gradual than for most other major American institutions.[4] We have no information on the Catholic Church specifically.

It is because of rising levels of education, changes in the Church, and growing skepticism toward institutions that Catholic church authority has been weakening. How much? Among which Catholics? We designed the Gallup surveys to see, giving our main attention to matters relating to sex and marriage because they are the ones on which feelings run highest today.

---

4. In Harris polls, the average decline in confidence for nine institutions (television news, medicine, the military, the press, organized religion, major companies, Congress, the executive branch, and organized labor) was 20 percentage points from 1966 to 1979, compared with about 14 points for organized religion alone. See *Public Opinion*, January 1980: 42. Another series of polls on confidence in institutions, running from 1973 to 1989, found a similar moderate decline for organized religion. See Richard G. Niemi, John Mueller, and Tom W. Smith, *Trends in Public Opinion: A Compendium of Survey Data.* New York: Greenwood Press, 1989: 105.

Moral Authority on Sex and Marriage Issues

In the interview we asked each respondent where ultimate moral authority regarding five issues *should* reside. We wanted to know how much moral authority he or she attributed to official church teachings as opposed to the voice of one's own conscience. Which can tell us about God's will? Here is the exact wording:

> Next, I would like your opinion on several issues that involve moral authority in the Catholic Church. In each case I would like to know who you think should have the final say about what is right or wrong. The choices are: A, the church leaders, that is, the pope and bishops; B, individuals taking church teachings into account and deciding for themselves; or C, both individuals and church leaders working together.

The three response options need to be explained. Option A seems quite clear. Option B seems moderately clear. It states that final moral authority rests with the individual Catholic after church teachings have been taken into account, and implies that specific decisions are meant here more than general moral principles or statements. Option C was not included in our initial interview design because we thought it too vague. It explicitly calls for the *sensus fidelium*, the common consent of the faithful, to have some influence. But how are church leaders and individuals to work together? If they work together, which should be more influential, and how should differences be overcome? Should they address general principles or specific situations? Option C pertains mainly to formulating general moral statements, not to making decisions on specific personal situations because in practice not enough people could investigate and attend to specific cases. Although option C is vague, we needed to include it in the final survey because in the 1987 pretests, *respondents demanded it*; we were told that church leaders and laity should *work together* and pool their wisdom for the good of everyone. Why decide between the two? Why not cooperate? Such a large number of respondents said this that we were convinced it represented a widespread attitude among Catholic laity.

Let us look at Catholic attitudes in 1987 and 1993 (Table 2.1). The five questions are rank-ordered according to how many people chose option A in 1987. In both years the most common response, averaged across all five topics, was B, "Individuals taking church teachings into account and deciding for themselves." The overall percentage choosing B was similar in 1987 and 1993.

Table 2.1
Locus of Final Moral Authority on Five Issues, 1987 and 1993

	1987 Options			1993 Options		
	A	B	C	A	B	C
Issue	Church Leaders (%)	Individuals (%)	Both (%)	Church Leaders (%)	Individuals (%)	Both (%)
Sexual relations outside of marriage	34	42	21	23	44	30
A Catholic who engages in homosexual behavior	32	39	19	26	39	30
A Catholic advocating free choice regarding abortion	29	45	22	21	44	33
A divorced Catholic remarrying without getting an annulment	23	31	43	23	38	37
A Catholic practicing contraceptive birth control	12	62	23	14	57	26

Note: "Don't know" percentages not shown.

The biggest shift in the six years was from option A to option C. On the first topic, sexual relations outside marriage, option A fell from 34 percent to 23 percent. On the second, homosexual behavior, it fell from 32 percent to 26 percent. And on the third, advocating free choice regarding abortion, it fell from 29 percent to 21 percent. On all three of these topics option C gained.[5]

5. A statistical note is needed here. Throughout the book we report no significance tests on data tables. This is done solely to make the text more readable and less complex. Nevertheless, we have carried out significance tests for all the trends and comparisons in the book, and we have adhered to the rule that we mention trends and relationships in the text only if they have been proven significant at the .05 level. This is the normal convention in data analysis. The reader may assume that any pattern in the data that we describe or emphasize has been checked and found to be significant. To illustrate the strength of relationships that are significant: when comparing the 1987 and 1993 NCR/Gallup surveys (whose sample sizes were 803 and 802), minimum differences in responses found to be significant at the .05 level are the following: for percentages in the range of 0-20 and 80-100, 4 percentage points; for percentages in the range of 20-80, 6 percentage points. When comparing smaller groups of, let us say, 250 cases in each, differences in the range of 0-20 and 80-100 need to be 7 percentage points and differences in the range of 20-80 need to be 11 percentage points. Any smaller changes may be due solely to sampling fluctuation.

Remarrying without getting an annulment and practicing contraceptive birth control did not shift, perhaps because many respondents had already chosen options B and C in 1987. The changes in attitudes from 1987 to 1993 occurred on the topics on which Catholics in 1987 had accorded the church leaders the most moral authority.

The main message to be derived from the data is that most Catholics see final moral authority as properly residing *with the individual or with a process involving both church leaders and the individual.* The proportion accepting binding authority from the institutional Church alone is small, never higher than 34 percent in 1987 and 26 percent in 1993.

Whatever explanation is best for the specific patterns, the trends over six years are consonant with other research. Usually attitude change is very slow on religious doctrinal issues, on the order of 1 percent or less a decade. But on more concrete institutional questions and moral topics, attitudes may change 1 percent a year or more. In our surveys, on the first three topics the trend averaged about 8 percentage points over six years; on the last two topics attitudes changed little.

Teachings on Church Authority and Conscience

Let us be clear about official church teachings on the question of final moral authority. Over the centuries the Church has developed a "teaching magisterium" on questions of morality, composed of the statements of popes and bishops (Komonchak, 1982; Congar, 1982). These statements are not all equally important but fall into two broad categories: infallible and non-infallible. Infallible statements are issued by popes on infrequent occasions and belong to the unchangeable body of doctrine. All others, by far the majority numerically, are non-infallible or "ordinary." No one asserts that they are free of error or that they state timeless truths incapable of change or development later.

Non-infallible church teachings demand deference and respect by the faithful. Church leaders declare that the teachings are closer approximations to the truth and the mind of God than can be gotten from any other source because they are carefully and prayerfully written by church leaders who are guided by the Holy Spirit. The body of non-infallible church documents is what option A in our question referred to. The documents themselves are numerous and difficult to read, hence few non-specialists in the Catholic community have studied them.

In the past two decades scholars have tried to correct misconceptions about the magisterium that many lay Catholics seem to hold today. They have made four arguments. First, as noted already, not all of the statements are infallible and in fact the vast majority are not. Second, although the documents themselves declare that they represent unchanging truths and that later formulations that apparently reverse earlier ones are really only "clarifications" and "developments," this is a fiction that cannot be maintained in light of the evidence. Official church teachings have changed within the past two centuries on slavery, church-state relations, ecumenism, authorship of books of the Bible, and other topics (Dulles, 1982; Noonan, 1993). Change in magisterial teachings is not a source of skepticism if one understands the nature and purpose of the teachings.

Third, non-infallible statements of the magisterium do not command full assent or obedience. They have definite authority but only in the sense of being the Church's best attempt to fathom the will of God at the time. A 1967 statement by German bishops explains:

> Since they are not *de fide* definitions, [the teachings] involve a certain element of the provisional even to the point of being capable of including error. . . . In such a case the position of the individual Christian in regard to the Church is analogous to that of a man who knows that he is bound to accept the decision of a specialist even while recognizing that it is not infallible. (Rahner, 1982:115)

That is, because the Holy Spirit is guiding the pope, the pope's pronouncements should be given a presumption in favor of their truly stating God's will. In some cases individual Christians may find the pronouncements unconvincing, and they are then morally bound to follow their inner convictions rather than submit to magisterial authority. According to the German bishops, faithful Christians in this situation are expected to study church teachings and to attempt to understand them fully. But beyond that they are not obligated to assent, and the dissent is legitimate. Arzube (1982:204) summarizes the teachings:

> Under what conditions, then, is dissent from ordinary church teaching legitimate? I submit, under the following conditions: 1. that those who dissent are competent to have an informed opinion on the matter; 2. that they have made a sincere and sustained prayerful effort to assent to the teaching; 3. that, despite such a sincere and sustained effort, the reasons for a contrary opinion remain so convincing as to make it truly impossible to assent.

Why would a Catholic dissent from a magisterial teaching? Usually because of a conflict between church authority and the person's conscience. Conscience is given considerable stature in Christian moral theology. It can be a valid expression of the Holy Spirit. The Apostle Paul described a natural law existing in all humans, whether Jew or Gentile: "What the law requires is written on their hearts, while their conscience also bears witness" (Romans 2:15). Thomas Aquinas developed the theory of Christian understanding of natural law and of conscience. Our main point here is that conscience is a valid basis for individual decision and action, and it is an important guide to moral behavior.

Yet conscience is not at all infallible. A well-formed conscience is a product of years of training, social experiences, and influences from family, teachers, and other responsible adults. One important part of forming conscience is the study of church teachings. Yet, even with these influences, not all human consciences are well formed. Some people develop overly strict consciences and some psychopathic people have no conscience at all. Therefore, conscience alone is not a reliable basis for action; it may be unduly shaped by bias, ignorance, selfishness, arrogance, or neurosis. Catholic theologians therefore insist that faithful believers constantly develop and inform their consciences so as to make them as mature and principled as possible (Fagan, 1987). An informed conscience has moral stature; an uninformed one does not.

The fourth and most important argument of scholars regarding misconceptions about the magisterium is that there is no clear consensus among theologians on which of the options in our question, A, B, or C, is the definitive church teaching. Theologians vary in emphasis. This statement may sound unconvincing to many Catholics. Many in the laity have agonized over problems of sexual ethics under the assumption that official church teachings demanded option A, that is, assent and obedience to official teachings of the magisterium. Numerous Catholics have felt a need to dissent on questions of birth control or divorce or whatever, but they sincerely believed they could not do so without endangering their salvation. Thus they conformed and continually felt unauthentic in doing so.

Although theologians differ, all agree that neither the non-infallible teachings of the magisterium taken alone nor the call of conscience taken alone can reliably discern what God wills. Both church teachings and conscience must be involved. A helpful paper by Avery Dulles summarized tradition on this question and tried to correct widespread misconceptions. He argued that past writers insisting that authority resides solely with the magisterium erred in not seeing the hand of the Holy Spirit in the community of faith. That point of view has no role for the *sensus fidelium*, the "sense of the faithful," whose importance was stressed by Vatican II.

Dulles wrote that the attention given in modern theology to the active role of the faithful is in many ways a welcome development. It corrects certain exaggerations to which the hierocratic model is prone – especially the unhealthy concentration of all active power in the hands of a small ruling class, with the corresponding reduction of the lower classes in the Church to a state of passivity scarcely consonant with lively Christian commitment (Dulles, 1982:252; also Dulles, 1988).

On the other hand, the *sensus fidelium* should not override all else either, and public opinion polls should not be touted as representing the sense of the faithful. In Dulles' words: "Not all in the Church are equally close to Christ and the Holy Spirit." Some Christians are unduly influenced by the mass media and the secular fashions of the day. Dulles says that to get the *sensus fidelium*, church leaders must keep in close communication with committed laity.

In Dulles' judgment the most defensible model of church authority today requires a combination of magisterium and conscience. Church leaders must try to discern the will of God, and the laity must do the same. Only when the two agree can church authority make itself fully felt (1982:252). Dulles espouses a pluralistic view of authority in the Church that, when properly understood, is close to option C in our surveys. Our surveys show that most Catholics over the age of 50 are deferential to the teaching magisterium and believe option A represents God's truth (more on this later). Many of these people are more reluctant to come to their own considered moral judgments than church teachings actually demand. In past decades in American parishes, thousands of pastors preached an overemphasis on the omniscience of the magisterium, and as Dulles says, this overemphasis needs some correction for good of the whole faith community. That is, the shift toward option C in our survey is in the proper direction.

Rights of the Laity in Church Decisions

Let us return to the surveys to look at several other questions related to church authority. The surveys included a series of questions asking whether the laity should or should not have the right to participate in church decisions, an issue at the heart of the tension between the hierarchical church structure and the democratic ambience in American culture. The issue has several complications, an important one of which is that church decisions vary in many ways, from local to international and from theological to pragmatic. For this reason the interviews asked about five areas of church decision making (see Table 2.2).

Table 2.2
Right of Participation by Laity in Church Decision-Making

Q.: For each of the following areas of church life, please tell me if you think the Catholic laity should have the right to participate, or should not have the right to participate.

	Should have the right	
	1987 (%)	1993 (%)
Deciding Local Parish Issues		
How income should be spent	81	83
Selecting the priest or priests	57	74
Deciding Institutional and Moral Issues		
Church policy on birth control	53	62
Church policy on divorce	50	61
Whether women should be ordained to the priesthood	48	62

Note: "Should not" and "Not sure" percentages not shown.

Each respondent was asked if he or she thought the Catholic laity should have the right to participate, or should not have the right to participate. The option of "don't know" was allowed and an average of 5 percent of the respondents chose it. The responses are numerically rank ordered in Table 2.2. The top two decision areas clearly were of a local-parish nature. The three decision areas on which the respondents were least likely to say that the laity should have the right to participate concerned broad institutional and moral issues: church policy on birth control, church policy about divorce, and whether women should be ordained to the priesthood. Average Catholics see the three issues as a bit more the clergy's business than the laity's. Stated differently, Catholic laypersons believe that they deserve a hand in *local, concrete* issues; they are less certain about deserving a hand in broader church issues and moral questions.

Six-year trends from 1987 to 1993 are all in the direction of saying that the laity should have the right to participate in church decisions. The topic on which attitudes shifted the most was parish-priest selection: an increase of 17 percentage points. The average increase in "should" was more than 10 percentage points, a strong trend for only six years. Probably the next six years will see more movement in the same direction.

The interview asked in another question, "Some people think the Catholic Church should have more democratic decision-making in church affairs that do not involve matters of faith than it has at the present time. Do you favor or oppose this idea?" (see Table 2.3) We included the key phrase "that do not involve matters of faith" because the pretest respondents demanded clarification of this point. As we have noted, many in the laity distinguish between practical institutional matters and central matters of doctrine.

Table 2.3
Desirability of More Democratic Church Decision-Making

Some people think the Catholic Church should have more democratic decision-making in church affairs that do not involve matters of faith than it has at the present time. Do you favor or oppose this idea?

	Favor	
	1987 (%)	1993 (%)
Parish level	60	61
Diocesan level	55	60
Level of the Vatican	51	58

Note: "Don't know" and "Oppose" percentages not shown.

We found that the majority of Catholics favored more democratic decision-making. The distinction they made in this regard among local, diocesan, and worldwide decision making was surprisingly small. In 1987, 60 percent wanted more democracy at the local parish level, 55 percent wanted more at the diocesan level, and 51 percent wanted more at the level of the Vatican. In 1993 the figures were slightly higher, but not enough to be statistically significant. The increases could be the product of sampling fluctuation, so we need to be cautious.

A question in a separate 1993 survey of Catholics (*USA Today*, 1993:6A) asked if rank-and-file Catholics should have more or less involvement in decision-making processes of the Church; 39 percent said "more"; 6 percent said "less"; and 49 percent said "same as now." This is more evidence of pressure toward democratization.

Another question in our 1987 and 1993 surveys asked whether the Catholic Church in the United States should become more independent from the Vatican and the Pope. It was asked because this topic is another indicator of the strength of church authority as accepted by American Catholics (see Table 2.4). The respondents had mixed opinions. About half thought the situation should remain as it is now; of the other half, more respondents asked for *more* independence than asked for *less* independence. (We seldom hear anyone in the United States advocating less independence from Rome, but this option was put into the interview for sake of balance.) The subject is apparently not one on which feelings run high, and there was little change in attitudes from 1987 to 1993.

Table 2.4
American Bishops' Relationship with the Vatican

Q.: Should the American bishops become more independent or less independent from the Vatican and the Pope in the way they run the Catholic Church in America, or should the situation remain as it is now?

	Favor	
	1987 (%)	1993 (%)
More independent	32	37
Less independent	10	11
Remain same as now	49	48

Note: "Don't know" percentage not shown.

Changes in Commitment and Confidence

The amount of church moral authority laypersons accept depends on their perceptions and experiences of church leadership. Have any changes taken place in recent years, either because of the underlying social processes or specific events in church life? For example, the pope has reaffirmed doctrinal control over Catholic theology as taught in Catholic colleges and universities, and this fact has been widely reported. Has this affected rank-and-file Catholics? Another example: the media have carried many stories of sexual misconduct by priests.

Has this news affected rank-and-file Catholics? The 1993 interview had three questions on change in the last five years (see Table 2.5).

Table 2.5
Changes in Layperson Commitment and Confidence

Q.: In the past five years, has your commitment to your local parish changed? Have you become more committed, less committed, or has there been no change? If you are not sure, tell me that.	
More committed	22%
Less committed	25
No change	50
Q.: In the past five years, has your confidence in the American bishops changed? Have you become more confident in them, less confident, or has there been no change?	
More confident	7%
Less confident	29
No change	63
Q.: In the past five years, has your confidence in the Pope and the Vatican changed? Have you become more confident in them, less confident, or has there been no change?	
More confident	13%
Less confident	16
No change	70

Note: "Don't know" percentage not shown.

The first question concerned commitment to one's local parish. The second and third concerned confidence in the American bishops, and in the Pope and Vatican. The most common response on all three was *no change*. Apparently, any overall change over five years was small. At the level of the bishops, confidence did decline overall: 29 percent of the respondents said they had become less confident, and only 7 percent said they had become more. At the level of the Pope and Vatican, there was little overall change. The only change in confidence over the past five years, if we can depend on the respondents' memories, was a drop in confidence in American bishops. The reason is not known.

In Sum

Catholics' views about church authority and religious authority affect many other areas of their lives. Those who believe in the official doctrines and teachings of the magisterium will have life commitments much different from those of others who do not, or who see church teachings as no more than one option among many. The data reviewed in this chapter suggest that American Catholics are according less authority to church teachings and more to their own consciences than in decades past. The people are gradually calling for more clergy-lay cooperation in moral teachings and more lay participation in church decision-making. In the future the laity will probably accept the Church's authority more readily if clergy-lay cooperation and lay participation increase.

Early in this chapter we said that strong church authority could be of inestimable value for everyone. A clear moral voice that cuts through ethnic, financial, and political rhetoric and speaks a salvific word to the whole world would be a blessing. If the Church's authority were strong, the world would listen, but recently the Church's authority has weakened. This has happened in part because of a divergence between church statements and the lived experiences of millions of laity. The *sensus fidelium* is different from some church teachings. Today the issue is whether the *sensus fidelium* contains revelatory wisdom and whether it has been adequately respected. Our findings indicate that paying more attention to it would probably bolster future church authority. As Avery Dulles suggested, some innovations to involve laity in discussions of moral issues would be wise.

References

Arzube, Juan. 1982. "Criteria for Dissent in the Church." In Charles E. Curran and Richard A. McCormick, (eds.), *Readings in Moral Theology No. 3.* New York: Paulist Press: 202-205.

Balz, Dan, and Richard Morin. 1991. "A Tide of Pessimism and Political Powerlessness Rises." *Washington Post*, 3 November.

Bianchi, Eugene C., and Rosemary R. Ruether. 1992. *A Democratic Catholic Church: The Reconstruction of Roman Catholicism.* New York: Crossroad.

Congar, Yves. 1982. "A Brief History of the Forms of the Magisterium and Its Relations with Scholars." In Charles E. Curran and Richard A. McCormick, (eds.), *Readings in Moral Theology No. 3.* New York: Paulist Press: 314-331.

Dolan, Jay P. 1987. *The American Catholic Experience: A History from Colonial Times to the Present*. Garden City, NY: Image Books.

Dulles, Avery. 1982. "Doctrinal Authority for a Pilgrim Church." In Charles E. Curran and Richard A. McCormick, (eds.), *Readings in Moral Theology No. 3*. New York: Paulist Press: 247-270.

________. 1988. "Authority and Conscience." In Charles E. Curran and Richard A. McCormick, (eds.), *Readings in Moral Theology No. 6*. New York: Paulist Press: 97-111.

Fagan, Sean. 1987. "Conscience." In *The New Dictionary of Theology*, ed. Joseph Komonchak, Mary Collins, and Dermot Lane. Wilmington, DE: Michael Glazier: 226-230.

Greeley, Andrew M. 1990. *The Catholic Myth: The Behavior and Beliefs of American Catholics*. New York: Scribner's.

_______, William C. McCready, and Kathleen McCourt. 1976. *Catholic Schools in a Declining Church*. Kansas City, MO: Sheed & Ward.

Hoge, Dean R. 1987. *The Future of Catholic Leadership: Responses to the Priest Shortage*. Kansas City, MO: Sheed & Ward.

Komonchak, Joseph A. 1982. "Ordinary Papal Magisterium and Religious Assent." In Charles E. Curran and Richard A. McCormick, (eds.), *Readings in Moral Theology No. 3*. New York: Paulist Press: 67-90.

Newsweek. 1967. "How U.S. Catholics View Their Church." 10 March: 68-75.

Niemi, Richard G., John Mueller, and Tom W. Smith. 1989. *Trends in Public Opinion: A Compendium of Survey Data*. New York: Greenwood Press.

Noonan, John T. 1993. "Development in Moral Doctrine." *Theological Studies* 54:662-677.

Public Opinion. 1980. Review of polls. January: 42.

Rahner, Karl. 1982. "The Dispute Concerning the Teaching Office of the Church." In Charles E. Curran and Richard A. McCormick, (eds.), *Readings in Moral Theology No. 3*. New York: Paulist Press: 113-128.

USA Today. 1993. "How U.S. Catholics View Their Church." 10 August: 6A.

Weber, Max. 1947. *The Theory of Social and Economic Organization*. Glencoe, IL: Free Press.

3

Human Sexuality

SHIFTS IN THE ATTITUDES AND BEHAVIOR OF THE CATHOLIC LAITY ARE seen most clearly on sexual issues. These issues have created tensions with church teachings that have been widely discussed in the media. To read newspapers today, a person would think that sexuality is all that is on the minds of Catholics, laity and hierarchy. In this chapter, we look more closely at church teachings on sexuality and how they are received by the laity. While most of the attention in the media and in church pronouncements seems to be about the evils of contraception, abortion, divorce, homosexuality and pedophilia, the Popes and bishops have in recent years also issued positive statements about human sexuality, marital love, and the family. Thus, it is a gross distortion to suggest that the Church's teachings are directed only on traditional morality.

We begin the chapter with an historical outline of church teachings about sexual matters and then examine trend data showing the attitudes and beliefs of the laity on these matters over the past thirty years. The theme of this chapter is that Catholics have developed a sense of sexual morality that draws its reasoning from the American ethos of personal autonomy and primacy of conscience. It also reflects personal experience based on a consequentialist ethic. This sense of morality is increasingly at odds with the official church pronouncements coming from the magisterium. Thus, if the sense of the faithful is meant to incorporate the beliefs of the laity as well as of the hierarchy (see *Lumen Gentium*, Chapter 12), our study shows that there is no universal agreement, no sense of the faithful, on these matters. To understand the growing disagreement, we begin with a brief review of the history of the Church's teachings and policies.

Human sexuality provides us with one of our greatest sources of pleasure – physical, social, psychological, and for many spiritual. It is also the means by which we assure the continuity of our species, and thus one of the ways by which we gain some degree of immortality. It has always been a central part of our being. But sexuality as pleasure and as the means of reproduction have had an uneasy relationship from the very beginning, to judge from the stories available to us from Scripture and history.

This uneasy relationship continues today, despite the work of the Papal Birth Control Commission, the more positive approach to sexuality found in the Encyclical *Humanae Vitae*, and the recent writings of John Paul II and the American bishops. One indication of the difficulties in opening a dialogue on human sexuality that would include the lived experience of the laity can be found in the efforts of the American Catholic Theological Society to establish such a dialogue. In 1977 the Paulist Press published *Human Sexuality*, the final report of a commission established in 1972 by the Board of Directors of the Catholic Theological Society of America. The Commission was charged with the responsibility to carry out a review of Catholic teachings and policies on human sexuality. The focus was primarily pastoral, with an awareness of the growing gap between Catholic teachings and contemporary sexual attitudes and behavior around the world. The writers used biblical, historical, empirical, and theological sources to address the central issues.

An indication of the difficulties the report would receive is found in the Foreword in which it was stated that:

> At the meetings of June 10 and October 15, 1976, the Board voted to "receive" the report and to arrange for its publication. These actions imply neither the approval nor disapproval by the Society or its Board of Directors of the contents of the report. The publication is intended as a service to the membership of the Society and a wider public of interested persons by making available the results of this research. The Board wishes to express its gratitude to the committee for its theological effort that promises to contribute to the further reflection and discussion that is called for on a topic of such moral and pastoral significance.

The authors hoped the report might lead to "an ever-deepening appreciation among all of God's people for the beauty, power and richness of the tremendous gift that is human sexuality" (p. XVI). Unfortunately, whatever its strengths and weaknesses, the report was withdrawn from publication within three years. The book was severely criticized by the American Catholic Bishops and was condemned by the Vatican's Congregation for the Doctrine of the Faith. The conflict arose over the attempt in the book to use empirical data from the lived experience of people to help rethink the ethical norms that should guide behavior. Thus, for example, the Vatican rejected the possibility that because most human beings masturbate in the process of growing to maturity, perhaps masturbation should not be seen as a sin, or at least a serious sin. Most important, an opportunity was lost to begin a dialogue on human sexuality that might bring the laity and magisterium toward a new level of understanding. To appreciate the growing gap between the laity and the magisterium, it is necessary to recall the historical sources for the magisterium's teachings.[1]

Sources of Church Knowledge and Teachings about Sexuality

The roots of the Judeo-Christian teachings about sexuality, especially love, fertility, masturbation, and contraception, are in the book of Genesis. The teachings are also grounded in other biblical texts, refined to some degree by Jesus during his lifetime, and further expanded by his apostles and church leaders through the ages. Their development reveals the never-ending interplay between attempts to expound universal principles and the time and culture context within which they occur. Here we cannot do justice to the richness and diversity of church writings on human sexuality, but the following points are central to our current understanding:

1. Sexuality is a *good* in itself, reflecting our mutuality, our belonging to one another. Thus, in the older Yahwist account of the creation (dating back to about 950 BC), we are told that God declared, "It is not good that man is alone; I will make him a helper like himself," (Gen. 2:18). Eve was created and the "two became one flesh."
2. Sexuality was not linked to procreation in biblical writings until some four hundred years later, when the Priestly account of creation was written (c. 587-500 B.C.) (Perry, 1992:2-5; Kosnik *et al,* 1977: 9). In that account, marriage was declared to be an arrangement

---

1. Despite its controversial nature, we found *Human Sexuality* useful for its presentation of the major historical events and writings on sexuality, and so we used it as a reference where relevant.

A new book published by Thomas C. Fox, *Sexuality and Catholicism,* presents a forceful, historical and theological overview of the Church's official and unofficial teachings on human sexuality through the centuries to the present time. It overlaps the Kosnick *et al* book, while providing important additional detail. Fox points to the impact of the Church's teachings, and the pain caused to the laity by them. Fox argues that the Church's survival in the 21st century depends on its ability finally to reconcile the lived experience of the laity, with the underlying truths of the Church's moral teachings, and Christ's message of love, caring, forgiveness, and reconciliation.

between families, not between a man and a woman. Fathers worked out the contracts. Thus, the biblical accounts, reflecting different historical circumstances, underwent a change from the original Genesis focus on the mutuality of sexuality to the focus on procreation as the prime purpose of sex.

3. The social purpose of marriage as clearly expressed in the contract was the begetting of children. This ideology fit well in an agricultural setting where a large family was vital to stability of the society. Sons were a guarantee that a man's name would not die out. The law of the Levirate (that a man should marry his deceased brother's childless widow) was instituted to protect the patriarchy. In this context, the story of Onan and Tamar is instructive. Tamar was married to Onan's brother, who died without heirs. The law required that Onan father a male heir by Tamar in order that his brother's name not die out in Israel. But Onan deceived Tamar and spilled his seed upon the ground to prevent any possible impregnation. Had he succeeded in his deceit, he would have stolen his brother's inheritance, embarrassed his brother's widow by leading villagers to think she was barren, and deprived her of her right to sexual pleasure. Contemporary scholars agree that Onan's sin was one of greed, selfishness, and deceit.
4. The Onan story (Gen. 38:8-10) had a tremendous influence on Christian teaching until recent times. It long provided the basis for Christian condemnation of masturbation and *coitus interruptus*. Christian churches used the story to condemn any form of contraception as well as masturbation. Catholic theologians no longer hold to this interpretation.
5. On the other side, the Old Testament's Song of Songs reveals a much more open, celebratory attitude toward human sexuality, emphasizing its joys and pleasures. Christian churches have not given much place to these themes until very recent times.
6. Jesus's teachings on sexuality were occasional and particular, not universal. St. Paul's teachings must also be seen in that context, focused specifically on life in the first century. It is agreed that Jesus saw law as an instrument to achieve well-being for the people. He saw women as equals, not as chattel. He did speak out against divorce, but in the context of protecting women from the dangers of a patriarchal society (Kosnik *et al*, 1977:17-29).
7. Paul thought Christ's return was imminent and prized celibacy above marriage. But he also understood that not everyone had the gift of celibacy, so he accepted the idea that marriage was better than being "aflame with passion." Paul also encouraged regular intercourse within marriage, as contrasted with other ascetics, who urged long periods of abstinence. But again, the emphasis in Paul was on the

impending Second Coming, for which people should be preparing, rather than spending too much time focused on this world.

8. Paul accepted Christ's teachings against divorce, but if a marriage between a Christian and non-Christian was not peaceful, Paul accepted that the Christian partner was no longer "bound," and could have the marriage dissolved and then remarry (1977:26).
9. On the other hand, Paul's letter to the Ephesians (5:22-33) on the nature of love was seen as a boon to marriage and has become a popular reading at wedding ceremonies. The essence of Christ's teaching had to do with love and equality. The symbolism of marriage as representative of the union of Christ and the Church can be understood as reflecting the union of husband and wife, of their becoming one flesh. Throughout most of early Christian history the symbolism was distorted by the patriarchal structures that dominated the Hebrew, Greek, and Roman cultures and that continue to influence Western culture.
10. During the second to fifth centuries, church leaders gradually institutionalized the teaching that marriage was a sacrament instituted by Christ. The period culminated with the work of Augustine, which came to dominate Christian thinking for the next 1,500 years. Augustine's sexual exploits as a young man influenced his thinking and writing in his later celibate years as priest, bishop, and theologian. Also in most of the centuries since Augustine, church leaders, writers, and related scholars have focused undue attention on the parts of Augustine's writings that related sexuality to original sin. Thus it was taught that sexuality was a good only insofar as it fulfilled its "natural" end, the procreation of children. In fact, the conjugal act was a duty to fulfill the end of procreation; only then was it sinless. Otherwise, an activity that could provide so much pleasure must be at least a little sinful. Augustine also fostered the idea of the fidelity of the couple to formal marriage vows, and that marriage itself was sacramental and hence indissoluble (Kosnik *et al*, 1977: 37).
11. In the Middle Ages, Thomas Aquinas gave order to church teachings on human sexuality, but did not fundamentally change anything. Based on the biological knowledge of the time, with its notion that the male seed was the active principle in the procreative process, it was not surprising that nothing much changed. Aquinas did teach that the conjugal act was a naturally good act.
12. Writers in the seventeenth to twentieth centuries did much to exaggerate the negative aspects of sexuality. With rapid urbanization, industrialization, and improved sanitation came increased numbers of people. Malthus warned about uncontrolled population growth, and worried that abstinence from sexual

intercourse, as the only legitimate means of controlling births, would not work. A movement arose first in France and then in England in the nineteenth century to control births through various forms of contraception. After years of discussion and disagreement, the Anglican bishops acknowledged in 1930 that contraceptive birth control could be morally acceptable. The Vatican responded at the end of the year with the encyclical *Casti Connubii*, which denounced contraception as intrinsically evil, thus setting the tone for Catholic teachings up to and through Vatican II.

13. Vatican II was an extraordinary experience of pluralism within the Roman Catholic Church. That pluralism was most manifest in the document *The Church in the Modern World*, which revealed a personalist-oriented theology of marriage and sexuality. Pluralism was further developed in the emphasis on religious freedom and the "responsibility for the determination of one's own life that has made the uncritical conformity to authoritative pronouncements an unacceptable response" . . . (Kosnik *et al*, 1977:49). Both *The Church in the Modern World* and the majority report of the Papal Birth Control Commission in 1967 rejected the primacy of procreation over conjugal love and at the same time gave "explicit recognition to the personal and interpersonal values at the core of human sexuality. They called attention to the human quality of expressions of sexuality and how they contribute to the growth and development of the person. They reflect a keen sensitivity to the social and communal dimensions of human sexuality and marriage" (Kosnik *et al*, 1977:50).

14. In July 1968, Paul VI rejected the majority report of the Papal Birth Control Commission. After praising the new insights into human sexuality and conjugal love, and the importance of responsible parenthood, he nevertheless reaffirmed the Church's traditional teachings. The crucial statement in his encyclical *Humanae Vitae* affirmed that "the Church, calling men back to the observance of the norms of the natural law, as interpreted by her constant doctrine, teaches that each and every marriage act must remain open to the transmission of life" (cited in Kosnik *et al*, 1977:48). The magisterium in its public statements and encyclicals since *Humanae Vitae* has persisted in declaring that every act of intercourse must be open to new life. Concurrently, Paul VI and now John Paul II have continued to explore a more personalist approach to human sexuality and have given positive expression to married love. But they have refused to rethink their teachings pertaining to masturbation, any form of non-marital sex, or any approach to fertility control other than what they have called natural family planning.

Research on the Present Situation

An abundance of social science data track the attitudes, beliefs, and practices of people throughout the world regarding matters of human sexuality. Changes in the attitudes, beliefs, and practices of American Catholics since the 1960s are common knowledge. We will show how age, education, gender, ethnicity, and level of commitment help us understand more clearly the trends and their implications for the future. It may be that many Catholics embrace the sections of *Humanae Vitae* that emphasize the goodness of conjugal love and the importance of responsible parenthood, especially in the sense of having smaller families. The greater probability is that today most Catholics know little or nothing of the content of *Humanae Vitae*. Their attitudes, beliefs, and practices are grounded in the general American ethos, ensuring an ever-widening gap between them and the magisterium.[2]

Briefly stated, the teachings of the magisterium are that non-marital sexual intercourse is always sinful, with or without the use of contraceptives; marital sex must always be open to procreation (thus allowing only the natural family planning method, or abstinence, as a licit means of birth control); marriage is indissoluble, except by death or annulment; and abortion is an absolute evil. The attitudes and practices of the Catholic laity vary greatly on these issues, and it is not helpful simply to conclude that the laity is in any kind of rebellion vis-à-vis the magisterium. Rather, laypersons in all age groups have been developing their attitudes, beliefs, and practices on the basis of personal experience influenced both by Vatican II (for the older age groups) and by events in their society. We examine four main topics: contraception, divorce and remarriage, non-marital sexuality including homosexuality, and abortion.

Contraception

Tim Unsworth (1994:13) quotes a forthright Catholic pastor: "Birth control is seen as the Pope's personal issue. For the rest of the faithful, it ranks with the flat-earth theory. Pastors simply don't mention

---

2. Greeley (1991) and Laumann *et al* (1994) present an impressive array of data on sexual practices in America that show Americans to be monogamous, satisfied with their sex life, and generally faithful to their partners. The findings from their studies do not support the picture of gloom and doom that is so often heard from religious conservatives. Future research may reveal the degree to which the Church's recent positive teachings on sexuality and marriage influence lay thinking, even if many traditional proscriptions are ignored.

it; the faithful never ask about it. Some priests feel the Pope has diluted his papal authority by his constant references to birth control in a world where children are born into disease and death." Although most of the faithful may never inquire into this subject and pastors may not bring it to their attention, survey researchers continue to pose questions having to do with it. The findings have not changed much in the past fifteen years, suggesting that a consensus was formed in the late 1970s and still obtains. As younger age cohorts mature, the probability is that they will feel little of the angst that their parents and grandparents felt about birth control.

Greeley (1993:18-21) made the point that contraception was a modern sin for most Catholics. He meant that throughout most of history discussions about contraception and abortion were carried on mostly at a philosophical and theological level, not at an everyday level. There were no letters to the laity admonishing avoidance of certain practices. Rather, the Church chose "not to disturb the consciences of the faithful," who had the more immediate concerns about poverty and survival to worry about.

Birth control became a non-issue as a result of the activities of the 1960s, for it was then that a majority of Catholics came to maturity as third and fourth generation Americans, mostly high school graduates and with an increasing number of college graduates. Studies showed that as late as the 1950s a majority of married Catholics professed to use rhythm (now called natural family planning) as their means of birth control, if they used anything. The decade of the 1960s was decisive in realigning their attitudes, beliefs, and practices. First, the "pill" became available over the counter beginning about 1960, and its mechanism of action was such that theologians were able to speculate about whether it might be acceptable within the traditional Catholic teaching framework. Then, during the early deliberations of Vatican II, Pope John XXIII removed the question from council deliberations and gave it to the Papal Birth Control Commission. When Paul VI succeeded John XXIII, he enlarged the commission to include some lay members, including Pat and Patty Crowley, chair couple of the worldwide Christian Family Movement. Discussion about the pill and its advantages as a contraceptive took place in the public domain, and Catholics participated in the debate, so the issue was hardly a private one for the commission.

A 1965 Gallup survey reported that 61 percent of the Catholic laity expected the Church to approve some kind of birth control method such as the pill, and 55 percent expected the approval to come within five years. That optimism perhaps resulted from the documents of Vatican II emphasizing freedom of conscience, plus rumors that the Papal Birth Control Commission was going to recommend a change in church policy.

A Harris/*Newsweek* survey of Catholics in 1967 found them still hopeful about a new official position, yet in the process of changing their own attitudes and practices. Consider the following responses to survey statements:

Believe church rules about birth control should be changed:	73%
Favor the Church's allowing use of birth control pills:	63
The rhythm method had failed to work for them:	54
Use the rhythm method for birth control in their marriage:	47
Favor the use of artificial birth control devices:	41
Had ever used an artificial birth control device in marriage:	27
Rhythm method works 75 percent or more of the time:	21
Had ever used birth control pills in their marriage:	19

Following the issuance of *Humanae Vitae* in July 1968, Gallup reported that 54 percent of the American Catholic laity who had heard about the encyclical opposed it, 28 percent favored it, and 18 percent had no opinion. Further, 65 percent of the respondents said it was possible to practice artificial birth control and still be a good Catholic. The 65 percent figure has changed little over time. In our 1987 and 1993 surveys, 66 percent and 73 percent respectively said one could be a good Catholic without obeying the Church's teaching on birth control. The most-loyal Catholics held the same view; in 1987 and 1993 majorities of Catholics who said they attended Mass every Sunday, who said the Church was one of the most important forces in their lives, and who said they would never leave the Church also said one could be a good Catholic without obeying the Church's teaching on birth control. (See Chapter 8 for a detailed discussion about the most-committed Catholics.)

In the 1987 and 1993 surveys we asked several other questions about birth control (see Chapter 2). One concerned who should have the right to decide on the morality of using contraceptive birth control; the options were church leaders alone, individuals alone, or both acting together. A majority said individuals alone, with only 14 percent in 1993 saying church leaders alone. And when we controlled for age, the percentages saying church leaders alone were small indeed. For the youngest cohort (18-34), only 9 percent supported the magisterium; the baby boomers (ages 34-54), were a bit more supportive, 13 percent; and those aged 55 and older were the most supportive, 22 percent.

Given that those over age 55 are less and less likely to have need for contraception, and that those still in the child-bearing years have few among them who look to the magisterium as the source of moral authority on this issue, it becomes evident why the pastor quoted above saw birth control as the Pope's issue.

Over the past three decades, the American Catholic laity has gradually come to a consensus on the matter of contraception. From the 1960s to the present there has been a steady movement away from simple obedience to church teachings. Because the matter of bringing children into the world is so intimately tied to sexual activity, it may not be surprising that the laity has reached consensus on this issue first among all the issues having to do with sexuality and marriage. In the matter of age at first marriage (now delayed until the late 20s) and number of births per family (now averaging two children), American Catholics now closely resemble their neighbors. This is another sign of the impact of assimilation and personal autonomy.

Divorce and Remarriage

Pre-Vatican II Catholics can still recall the negative impact of divorce on Catholic family life. Indeed, divorce and remarriage were much more visible among family and neighbors than was the purchase and use of contraceptives, and they carried a much higher level of stigma. By the 1960s divorce rates among Catholics were beginning to approach those of Protestants, and the Harris/*Newsweek* 1967 survey of Catholics also found evidence that Catholics were expecting change here, as they were in other matters relating to human sexuality. That year Catholics gave these responses:

They would favor the Church's allowing Catholics to divorce	40%
They would favor the Pope's allowing an annulment of a marriage having one innocent party	65
They would not be upset were the Pope to annul certain marriages	75

With divorce and remarriage becoming ever more common in the late 1960s and 1970s, Catholics moved away from the orthodox church teaching. By 1979, Joan L. Fee and colleagues (1981:18) reported that among American Catholics aged 18-29, only 11 percent disagreed with the statement that it was okay for divorced people to remarry if they were in love.

In the 1992 survey, 72 percent of the Catholics said divorced and remarried Catholics should be allowed to receive communion. And in 1993, only 23 percent said that the magisterium alone should have the final say in deciding on the morality of a divorced Catholic's remarrying without having received an annulment from the Church. The figures among younger Catholics again remind us how much change is taking place as different cohorts move through the life cycle. In the CFFC 1993 survey, 87 percent of young Catholics said that remarriage after divorce could be a morally acceptable act. Even among the Church's most committed Catholics in the Gallup 1993 survey (those who say they go to Mass every week, that the Church is one of the most important forces in their lives, and that they would never leave the Church), 44 percent said that one could be a good Catholic without obeying the Church's teaching on divorce and remarriage.

Divorce and remarriage are approaching non-issue status for many priests. Unsworth's comment on one pastor's reflections on divorce is instructive here. Referring to his reading of Bowman's study of Chicago pastors, Unsworth (1994:13) states: "Perhaps the greatest amount of rule-bending reported in Bowman's survey concerns problems involving marriage. . . . 'We run our own chancery office [regarding marriage],' one pastor said. 'All [marriage] cases should be handled at the parish level. We should get out of the marriage business.'" Unsworth added: "He sounded a bit strong, but his response represents the majority view. He had simply grown tired of inviting people to join the Church, learning that they were in a second marriage, and having to inform them that the church door was blocked until they could get an annulment."

With recent statistics (Greeley, 1991:35) showing that at least half of the baby-boomer generation has been divorced, we may expect that Catholic baby boomers will be no different from their peers in this respect. This is the first Catholic generation to be committed to contraception as a moral practice, and it is also a generation known for lower church attendence than previous generations. So we may expect that divorce and remarriage will be resolved either by the couple's leaving the Church, or as the above-quoted pastor indicated, by parish priests bending the rules. In some cases, at least, the priests will be doing so in defiance of the Pope and their bishops. For example, the seventeen bishops of Pennsylvania issued a letter to their priests rejecting the idea "that divorced Catholics living in an unsanctioned second marriage can receive communion [unless] they seek to live in complete continence" (reported in *National Catholic Reporter,* 12 August 1994:6). This was followed in October by a more definitive statement from the Pope himself (reported in *NCR,* 28 October 1994:10): "If the divorced are remarried civilly, they find themselves in a situation that objectively contravenes God's law. Consequently, they cannot receive holy communion as long as this situation persists." The statement forced the German bishops to end their policy of tolerating the receiving of communion by divorced and remarried Catholics.

Non-Marital Sexuality

The long history of the Church's condemnation of masturbation, homosexuality, extra-marital sexuality, and pre-marital sexuality are well known to all pre-Vatican II Catholics. Clergy spend very little time these days preaching about masturbation. Just about all males and a majority of females masturbate (Kosnik *et al*, 1977:57), and there is no evidence of physical or psychological harm when it is a normal part of adolescent development. While it is difficult to see what positive value accrues from declaring masturbation to be sinful behavior, the magisterium continues to do so, as Pope John Paul II did in his encyclical *Veritatis Splendor* (October, 1993). For most people, it is another non-issue. However, two key aspects of human sexuality that continue to be issues are pre- and non-marital heterosexual and homosexual behavior.

Fee and colleagues (1981:18) found that by 1979 only a minority (17 percent) of young Catholics 18-29 supported the official Catholic teaching that premarital sexual relations were almost always or always wrong. Given the dramatic changes in attitudes and probably also in behavior during the late 1960s and early 1970s, these figures should not be surprising. That period has come to be known as the time of the sexual revolution. Most of the empirical data suggest that changes in behavior began after World War II. If there was a revolution, it was in the attitudes, beliefs, and values of the young. That is, as more and more young people engaged in premarital sexual activity, their attitudes toward the teaching that it was a serious sin began to change.

A Princeton Religion Research Center report (October 1993:2) stated that "Catholics under 50 (60 percent) are twice as likely as those older (30 percent) to disagree that it is always wrong to have sex outside of marriage. By the same margin, younger Catholics are more likely to believe one can have sex outside of marriage and still be a good Catholic." The findings from our 1987 and 1993 studies provide further support for this attitude: In the six years, the percentage of Catholics who said that church leaders alone should have the authority to decide the morality of sexual relations outside marriage dropped from 34 percent to 23 percent, while the percentage who said that it was a matter for individuals alone remained stable at 42 to 44 percent; the increase during this time period was in the category "church leaders and individuals together."

Pre-marital sexual relations are rapidly becoming a non-issue; this is shown in attitudes of young Catholics in the CSO 1992 survey. Sixty-eight percent of the entire sample agreed (somewhat or strongly) that pre-marital sexual relations between persons who are committed to each other can be morally acceptable; among Catholics under 35, fully 86 percent agreed. And in our 1993 survey, among Catholics under 35, only 17 percent said that the church leaders alone should have the final say about the morality of sexual relations outside marriage. Even among Catholics over age 55, only one in three supported that position.

In whatever way we ask about the morality of pre-marital relations, the trend line is clear and has been for more than twenty years. In trying to come to grips with this new reality, the Catholic Theological Society of America's commission made the following observations: "The Old Testament does not contain a prohibition against premarital intercourse as such but primarily against the promiscuity typified by intercourse with prostitutes." And further, the New Testament "explicitly condemns completely unhampered sexual intercourse, i.e., relations with prostitutes" (Kosnik *et al*, 1977: 154-155).

The report concluded, "There can be no doubt but that the traditional moral code regarding premarital sex is inadequate, particularly in its lack of distinction between the ages, attitudes and intentions of the people involved. The alternative, however, is not simply moral relativism or the surrender of human values, Christian ideals, or ethical norms" (Kosnik *et al*, 1977:167). Our data suggest that if the magisterium wishes to influence the coming generation of young people, it will need to engage in serious dialogue with the laity and with the theologians representing the full spectrum of thinking on this subject. We believe that if these issues are not approached in a way that meaningfully involves laity and theologians, the moral authority of the magisterium will continue to erode.

Homosexuality

Perhaps the only area in which a trend away from absolute proscription is not so clear is homosexuality. The CTSA's commission report reminds us that "nowhere has homosexual activity been viewed with as much abhorrence as in the Judeo-Christian West. Neither Islam nor Hinduism sees it as taboo. Primitive peoples like the Eskimos, Malaysians, and North American Indians had no difficulty accepting it; ancient Greece institutionalized it. In some primitive cultures, a homosexual was even seen as a kind of shaman or holy man, certainly not as a criminal" (Kosnik *et al*, 1977:188). Homosexuality, then, is as old as human sexuality, and seems to exist in all societies. Evidence suggests that exclusively homosexual activity among males has hovered at under the 10 percent level and for females at under the 2 percent level (Pierson and D'Antonio, 1974: 270-271; Kosnik *et al*, 1977:70-74; Laumann et al, 1994). Whether homosexuality is the result of genetic, social, psychological, or other factors is still undetermined. The sexual revolution has brought both change and resistance within the Church and civil society. In some ways, attitudes about homosexuality remain more narrowly circumscribed than about abortion. Trend data for the period 1973-1988 (Niemi, *et al,* 1989:195) show that attitudes of the general population have remained very stable and highly negative; the percentages of Americans saying homosexual behavior is always wrong ranged between 70 and 74 percent in the annual General Social Surveys (GSS).[3]

Attitudes of the Catholic laity toward homosexuality have been measured by a variety of questions during recent years. The results suggest that Catholics are becoming more tolerant on the matter. For example, Fee and colleagues (1981) stated that young Catholics and Protestants (18-29) were pretty much in agreement (77 percent of Catholics and 73 percent of Protestants) that homosexual relations were almost always or always wrong. These figures correspond with the national findings of the GSS reported above.

By 1992, however, Catholic attitudes were changing; 45 percent of the Catholics in the 1992 survey said that "sex relations between gay and lesbian persons in a committed relationship can be morally acceptable." Forty-nine percent disagreed, and 6 percent were unsure. Note the wording of the statement. It specifies "committed relationship"

---

3. The sample size (N) ranged from 1,531 in 1985 to 973 in 1988, with the majority around 1,485 (Niemi *et al*, 1989:195). Differences between men and women were minimal.

and whether such a relationship *can be* morally acceptable. Level of support seems to decline when the wording is more general as it was in the 1993 CFFC survey statement, "Gay and lesbian relations can be morally acceptable." Only 26 percent of the men and 28 percent of the women agreed with that statement.

Our 1987 and 1993 surveys asked a number of different questions. First, we wanted to ascertain where the laity thought the moral authority to decide on such issues as homosexuality should reside. This question makes no assumptions about whether the laity knew anything about the Church's formal teachings. The results are presented in Table 3.1.

Table 3.1
Regarding Homosexual Behavior

Q: Does moral authority regarding homosexual behavior lie with Church leaders alone?

		Yes	
		1987 (%)	1993 (%)
Sex			
	Men	31	32
	Women	33	21
Age			
	18-34	25	22
	35-54	29	27
	55+	47	30
Geographic Region			
	East	35	24
	Midwest	26	25
	South	38	27
	West	29	29

Note: "No" percentages not shown.

A dramatic change occurring between 1987 and 1993 was in the attitudes of women. There was a significant drop (12 points) in the percentage of Catholic women looking to church leaders alone for guidance. And, one in three men in both 1987 and 1993 said that moral authority should lie with church leaders alone.

Again, with regard to age, the significant change came among Catholics 55 years and older. In 1987 almost half said the morality should be determined by church leaders alone; in 1993 only 30 percent gave that response. Meanwhile, among the youngest Catholics, the percentage looking to church leaders dropped below 25 percent.

Finally, we found in both surveys that less than 30 percent of Catholics in the Midwest and West said that the moral authority should rest with church leaders alone. Catholics in the East and South gave significantly different responses between 1987 and 1993, bringing them into close conformity with Catholics in the Midwest and West. For many years now, the West has been the trend-setting area of the country, with new norms of personal behavior usually taking root there, and the East and South have been more traditional bastions of support for the old norms. At least on the question of the locus of the morality of homosexual behavior, there is consensus emerging in all four regions.

Abortion

Abortion has enjoyed much more legal protection in Western nations than has homosexuality. And the theological underpinnings against abortion in the Bible and early Christian Scriptures are much more ambiguous than are those for homosexuality. At the same time, the religious literature has often been strident in opposition to abortion. In this section, we provide a brief historical review of the main factors in the debate as background for the discussion of recent survey data.

Christian opposition to abortion was grounded in the commitment to Jesus' commandment of love that makes the taking of life a forbidden act. Thus, from the first century onward, abortion has been condemned as a serious sin on grounds that it destroys what God has created and constitutes "an offense to a necessary love of neighbor" (Callahan, 1970:410). The condemnation was gradually elaborated upon but by the twelfth century a distinction was being made between abortions performed before ensoulment and those performed after (Callahan, 1970:411). This led to attempts by theologians during the next several centuries to develop norms that might allow for therapeutic abortions when the mother's life was in danger; however, none was ever arrived at, and by the nineteenth century, the papacy had taken more and more control over the abortion issue. As abortion became more prevalent in the nineteenth and early twentieth centuries, "the papacy took the lead in condemning abortion at all stages, denying any exceptions and erasing the distinction between a formed (ensouled) and unformed fetus" (Callahan, 1970:413; Burns, 1992).

The Church's stand was made clear in the encyclical *Casti Connubii* (1970:417) in 1930 and has been reaffirmed by every Pope since then. Callahan (1970:417) summarized the Church's position:

(1) God alone is the Lord of Life.

(2) Human beings do not have the right to take the lives of other (innocent) human beings.

(3) Human life begins at the moment of conception.

(4) Abortion, at whatever the stage of development of the conceptus, is the taking of innocent human life.

The conclusion follows: Abortion is wrong. The only exception to this conclusion is in the case of an abortion which is the indirect result of an otherwise moral and legitimate medical procedure (e.g., the treatment of an ectopic pregnancy and cancerous uterus).

The central issue seems to rest on the principle that human life begins at conception. In what sense is the embryo a human being endowed with such sacred qualities that no one can interfere with its development to term? By declaring that human life begins at conception and that it is innocent, and therefore cannot be subject to abortion, the magisterium has taken its stand, and even in the face of disagreement from other religious denominations has refused to move from it.

It is this stance taken as public policy that seems most to conflict with the ethos of pluralistic democracy, a tolerance for uncertainty, and personal autonomy as it has emerged in the assimilation process in the United States. What has also emerged, and perhaps is of more importance, is a change in the thinking of many Catholics. The Church in the person of the Pope has upheld the traditional teaching, but the Church in the persons of some lay counselors and many laity has promoted the consequentialist view that abortion's rightness or wrongness is related to the circumstances and their impact on the people involved. They may be interpreting the impact in terms of relative suffering, sense of injustice, and the meaning of life. Our examination of the data on abortion helps us understand the degree to which the laity does and does not continue to support the teachings of the magisterium, or is found to be leaning more and more toward a consequentialist perspective.

We begin with a summary of the GSS surveys covering the period 1962-1988. Questions dealing with the conditions under which a woman might seek an abortion appear in Figure 3.1.

Figure 3.1
Percentage of American Population Supporting a Woman's Right to Abortion Under Six Conditions, 1962-1988

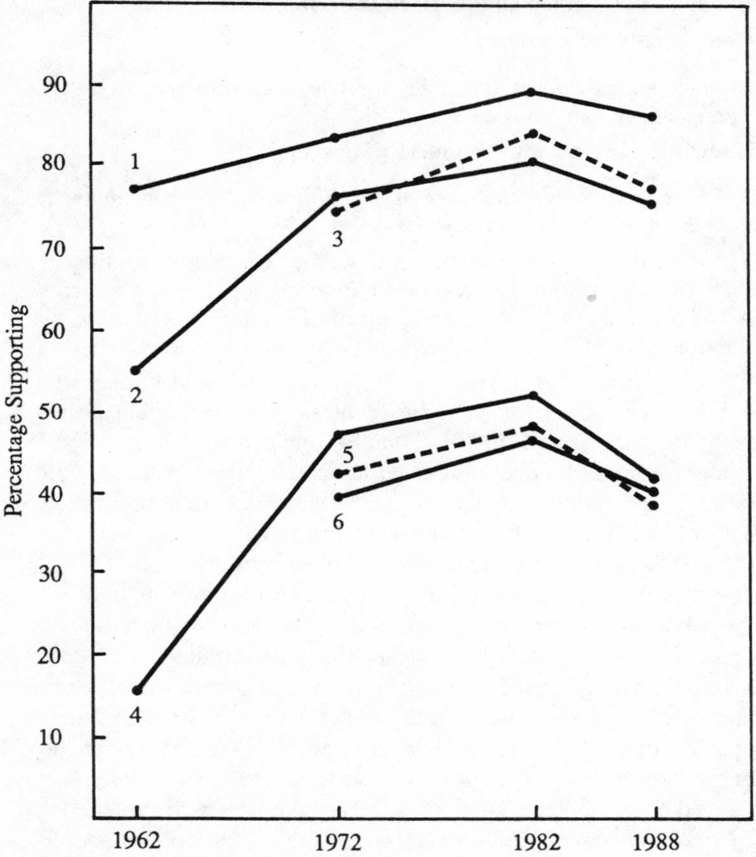

Legend: 1 Woman's Health
2 Birth Defect
3 Rape
4 Family Has Low Income
5 Woman Not Married
6 Woman Wants No More Children

Source: *Trends in Public Opinion,* p. 89.

The first three possible abortion situations are called the "hard" cases, and over time a consensus has emerged in support of abortion for women whose health is endangered by a pregnancy, whose pregnancies have a high probability of infant birth defects, and whose pregnancies are the result of rape. Fee and colleagues (1981) reported that only 15 percent of young Catholics and Protestants opposed a legal abortion where there was a chance of a serious birth defect. There is maximum consensus supporting the right to abortion when a woman's health is endangered (Figure 3.1). Support for the other two hard cases is close to the 80 percent level, with Protestants and Catholics agreeing.

The second three conditions, known as "soft" cases, have consistently elicited much less support for abortion. The most notable differences have been among Catholics, as seen, for example, in connection with conditions in which a married woman does not want any more children. Fee and colleagues (1981) reported that 51 percent of young Catholics, compared with 56 percent of young Protestants, opposed abortion in such instances. In the GSS data for 1988, only 39 percent of the total sample supported a woman's right in this situation (41 percent of Catholics and 33 percent of Protestants). Over time, Protestant opinion has remained stable while there has been increasing Catholic support. These findings from other surveys are consistent with the discussion in the previous chapter on the laity's changing stance on the locus of moral authority.

Consistent with the above findings, about one-third of all Americans have supported the right to abortion for a woman for any reason whatsoever (Niemi, *et al*, 1989:212). On the other side, Americans have also been fairly consistent in the percentage saying that abortion should never be legal; about 20 percent generally take that position (Niemi, *et al*, 1989:213). The findings from the CSO 1992 survey are generally supportive of these trends, with some refinements (see Table 3.2).

As expected, Catholics over age 55 in 1992 and those who attended Mass at least weekly were the most likely to adhere strictly to the teaching of the magisterium on abortion, yet even they failed to give it majority support. Indeed, a higher percentage (31 percent) said that abortion should be legal in many or all cases than said that abortion should never be legal (21 percent). Almost the same percentages held for Catholics who said they attended Mass at least weekly. Further, in response to a separate question, 70 percent of all Catholics agreed that Catholics could in good conscience vote for political candidates who supported legal abortion.

The 1992 survey also attempted to distinguish between the legality of abortion and abortion as a moral choice. Responses to the question "Do you believe abortion can be a morally acceptable choice?" were

Table 3.2
Catholic Lay Opinion on Legality of Abortion (1992).

	All Catholics	Age			Church Attendance		
	(%)	<35 (%)	35-54 (%)	55+ (%)	Weekly (%)	Occasional (%)	S/N (%)
Illegal in all circumstances	13	9	11	21	22	8	6
Legal only rarely	33	29	29	45	45	29	21
Legal in many or all cases	52	60	58	31	31	61	70

Source: "Catholics Speak Out" survey, April-May 1992.

as follows: never: 13 percent; only rarely: 41 percent; in many circumstances: 26 percent; in all circumstances: 15 percent; and don't know/no opinion: 5 percent.

As expected, Catholics 55 and older and those who attended Mass at least weekly were most likely to restrict the conditions under which abortion might be a moral choice, and they had the highest percentages (18 percent and 22 percent, respectively) saying that abortion could never be a morally acceptable choice.

Further evidence of the persistence of a Catholic lay position in support of abortion and in opposition to magisterial teaching was found in our 1987 and 1993 surveys: "Can a person be a good Catholic without obeying the Church's teaching regarding abortion?" In 1987, 39 percent said yes; in 1993, 56 percent.

The abortion debate has been very divisive for religious Americans. The issue was joined not only by the now-famous *Roe v. Wade* Supreme Court decision of 1973 but also by the fact that during the past thirty years the Protestant churches have split among themselves on the legal and moral aspects of abortion. Most of the mainline churches (Presbyterian, Methodist, Episcopalian, American Baptist, and United Church of Christ, among others), have made formal statements supporting the right to abortion at least under the hard conditions noted above. A majority of the Catholic laity has moved in their direction. The Catholic Church hierarchy and a small but highly committed minority of the laity have been joined by the Southern Baptists, the Mormons, and a number of other fundamentalist denominations and sects in opposition to abortion. The great majority of American

Jews continue their longstanding support of the right to abortion. Islamic scholars are split over the issue.

Burns (1992:200-208) argues that attempts by the bishops and the Pope to make abortion strictly a moral issue subject to religious sanction, and to insist that abortion should not have governmental protection, threaten the hard-won gains made by the American bishops as legitimate participants in the political arena. In the United States, abortion is a political issue. With the Catholic laity clearly at odds with the magisterium on abortion, and supporting the legality of abortion under at least some conditions, the issue seems certain to continue to be divisive both within and outside the Catholic Church.

Conclusion

The findings from a range of surveys reported in this chapter strongly suggest that the American Catholic laity is evolving a new sexual morality, much of it without benefit of the Church's teaching authority. This morality is consonant with the moral norms that have been evolving with the majority of Americans as attested by surveys and reports throughout the past thirty years. The Catholic Theological Society report reflected on this evolving morality and on the traditions from which it is gradually separating. We have noted that that report was heavily criticized and finally condemned by the Vatican, then withdrawn from publication. Still, there is much of value in it.

Under the present circumstances in the American Catholic Church, the most that we might hope for is a continuing effort by theologians to study the empirical evidence on sexual behavior and attitudes, and reflect on them in light of their discipline. The bishops for their part may be expected to give emphasis to the importance of conjugal love and responsible parenthood, while trying to find ways to convey the traditional moral teachings to three generations of Catholics. We turn our attention now to a detailed examination of the attitudes and beliefs of these three generations.

References

Burns, Gene. 1992. *The Frontiers of Catholicism: The Politics of Ideology in a Liberal World*. Berkeley: University of California Press.

Callahan, Daniel. 1970. *Abortion: Law, Choice, and Morality*. New York: Macmillan.

D'Antonio, William V., James D. Davidson, Dean R. Hoge, and Ruth Wallace. 1989. *American Catholic Laity in a Changing Church*. Kansas City, MO: Sheed & Ward.

Fee, Joan L., Andrew M. Greeley, William C. McCready, and Teresa A. Sullivan. 1981. *Young Catholics in the United States and Canada*. New York: William H. Sadlier Co.

Fox, Thomas C. 1995. *Sexuality and Catholicism*. New York: George Braziller.

General Social Surveys. 1985, 1988.

Greeley, Andrew M. 1991. *Faithful Attraction*. New York: TOR.

________. 1993. "Contraception: A Baby Among Church's Sins," *National Catholic Reporter*, 15 October: 18-21.

Hadaway, Kirk, Penny Long Marler, and Mark Chaves. 1993. "What the Polls Don't Show: A Closer Look at U.S. Church Attendance," *American Sociological Review*, 58:6 (December): 741-752.

Kosnik, Anthony, William Carroll, Agnes Cunningham, Ronald Modras, and James Schulte. 1977. *Human Sexuality*. New York: Paulist Press.

Laumann, Edward O., John H. Gagnon, Robert T. Michael and Stuart Michaels. 1994. *The Social Organization of Sexuality*. Chicago: University of Chicago Press.

Niemi, Richard G., John Mueller, and Tom W. Smith. 1989. *Trends in Public Opinion*. New York: Greenwood Press.

Perry, John M. 1992. *Exploring the Genesis Creation and Fall Stories*. Kansas City: Sheed & Ward.

Pierson, Elaine Mastroianni, and William V. D'Antonio. 1974. *Female and Male: Dimensions of Human Sexuality*. Philadelphia: Lippincott.

Schoenherr, Richard, and Lawrence A. Young, 1993. *Full Pews and Empty Altars*. Madison: University of Wisconsin Press.

Unsworth, Tim. 1994. "Parish Priests Cope with Mess: Chanceries Tangled up in Rules," *National Catholic Reporter*, 20 May: 13.

4

Three Generations of Catholics: Pre-Vatican II, Vatican II, and Post-Vatican II

THREE GENERATIONS OF LAYPEOPLE EXIST IN TODAY'S AMERICAN Catholic Church: pre-Vatican II Catholics, Vatican II Catholics, and post-Vatican II Catholics (Davidson and Williams, 1993; Williams and Davidson, 1994). Pre-Vatican II Catholics were born in the 1910s, 1920s, and 1930s; their formative (teenage and young-adult) years were in the 1930s and 1940s. They matured well before Vatican II. Vatican II Catholics were born in the 1940s and 1950s and experienced the 1950s and 1960s in their formative years. They have one foot in the "old Church" (before Vatican II) and one in the "new Church" (after Vatican II). Members of the post-Vatican II generation were born in the 1960s and 1970s and came of age in the 1970s and 1980s. All they've ever known in the religious sense is the post-Vatican II Church.

In some respects, these generations are similar to birth cohorts examined in other recent studies of American generations (Walrath, 1987; Roof, 1993; Hoge, Johnson, and Luidens, 1994). However, these three Catholic generations are not just the result of societal forces; they are defined by their relationship to a specifically Catholic event: Vatican II (1962-1965). The Church has played a major role in shaping their religious perspectives (McNamara, 1993). In this chapter we explain our view of generations, describe the different ways in which the three generations of Catholics were reared, and then show that their formative experiences have produced very different ideas of what it means to be Catholic.

Generations

Sociologists have long argued that experiences during one's formative years (especially traumatic experiences, such as the Great Depression of the 1930s and the protests of the 1960s) produce solidarity among members of one generation and mark them off from members of other generations. Their experiences foster generation-based social relationships and world views that are very different from those of other generations (Mannheim, 1952).

Members of generations use the social relationships and world views developed during their formative years to make sense of the experiences they have in later stages of their lives. In Walrath's (1987: 35-38) words:

> They move chronologically through childhood, youth, and so forth on into old age like the generations that preceded them. But their experiences of the world are qualitatively very different at similar life stages. . . . They never let go of the experienced differences. . . . They continue to perceive and define the world in terms of that unique framework as they progress throughout their lives. They perceive the same experiences differently from those socialized previously, who are now side by side with them in the same period. In important respects they never grow up to take on the same perspectives their elders held.

Generation-defining experiences have lifelong effects. Although members of all generations age and pass through essentially the same life cycles, members of each generation age and experience the life cycle variously. As a consequence of their dissimilar religious backgrounds, pre-Vatican II, Vatican II, and post-Vatican II Catholics are likely to have very different views of the Church throughout their lives, even when they are at the same age or stage in life as the generations immediately before and after them.

Three Generations of Catholics

We'd like you to meet members of coauthor James Davidson's family: his Irish Catholic mother, Louise (a member of the pre-Vatican II generation), Jim (who belongs to the Vatican II generation), and Jim's two kids, Jay and Terry (both reared in the post-Vatican II era).

Louise: A Pre-Vatican II Catholic

Louise Fitzpatrick was born in 1907, the daughter of Irish immigrants, and grew up in a small town in western Massachusetts. About half the people in her hometown were Catholic, and it seemed as though half of them were relatives. The people in Louise's family had names like Patrick Fitzpatrick and Delia Sweeney Fitzpatrick (Louise's parents); George Fitzpatrick (Louise's brother), Eileen McArdle Fitzpatrick, and their children Marjorie, Pat, and Mike; and Theresa Fitzpatrick (Louise's sister), her husband James Welch, and their daughter Margaret. Louise's relatives had last names like Sweeney and Walsh. How Irish can you get?

Think of the world Louise grew up in. As recent immigrants, her parents and relatives knew anti-Catholicism firsthand. They were close to one another, but being strangers in someone else's land (for example "no Irish need apply") produced even more togetherness. The whole family would gather for singing and dancing on St. Patrick's Day. Here's how Louise recalled her Irish upbringing in a recent letter to her son Jim:

> Thank you for my pretty St. Patrick's day card. I will keep it as I like the verse on it. . . . We used to have such good times at home – Papa's birthday and George and Eileen playing music. I can even remember when I was very young and my parents had kitchen dances. Aunt Annie would play the accordion and Papa the flute. Father Murphy would have a high Mass, and the choir would sing 'All Praise to St. Patrick.'

Louise's father became a chauffeur, then started a milk-processing plant, which he later passed on to his son George. He also bought three houses, which he gave to his children. Louise's mother stayed home and raised four kids. After high school, Louise could have gone to a nearby Catholic women's college, but she chose to stay in her hometown, working in a local store as a bookkeeper. Louise experienced the "Roaring Twenties" and then the economic depression of the 1930s during her formative years. In 1941 she married an Episcopalian named James Davidson (the coauthor's father). It was not long before he was drafted into the army and sent to France during World War II. Louise and her new baby, Jim Jr., lived with her sister Theresa and Theresa's new daughter, Margaret, while their husbands were at war. When Louise's husband returned, they had a second son, John.

Louise was raised in the "old Church," where she learned that the Pope, bishops, and priests were set apart from (holier than) laypeople. She looked up to pastors like Father Murphy and Father Kerrigan;

everyone did. She was taught that the Church was "the one true Church" and that she was to comply with its teachings. And she did. She dutifully took her family (including her Episcopalian husband) to church every Sunday, on all of the Holy Days, and on other occasions such as Stations of the Cross, Forty Hours Devotions, and Benediction on Sunday nights. Every night before going to sleep, Louise would read prayer cards; she still does. She prayed fervently that her husband would become a Catholic, which he did much later, after his mother died. Louise remembers her parish's being packed with young families during the 1950s. Sunday school classes were huge; First Communion and Confirmation involved hundreds of kids, all dressed to the hilt in white outfits.

Louise's Son Jim: A Vatican II Catholic

Louise's oldest son, Jim, was born in 1942. His teenage years included the baby boom of the 1950s. There were kids all over the neighborhood, always playing games – baseball in summer, football in the fall, basketball in winter. Jim went to the same public high school his mother and father had attended. By the 1950s, the school's administration and faculty included numerous Catholics. Most of his closest friends were Catholic, but one was a Congregationalist and another a Jew. His formative years included the euphoria of John Kennedy's election as the country's first Catholic president; a distant awareness of a civil rights movement in the South; the assassination of John Kennedy; LBJ, the Great Society, and the War on Poverty; going to a Catholic undergraduate school (Fairfield University) and a Catholic graduate school (University of Notre Dame); the assassinations of Bobby Kennedy and Martin Luther King; social conflict over Vietnam; and settling down in the Midwest.

Jim's Irish Catholic mother made sure that he learned the importance of being Catholic. He, too, looked up to the priests in the parish; respected the nuns he had for Sunday school; learned about the faith by memorizing the Baltimore Catechism; became an altar boy; attended all the Masses and devotional activities his mother went to; sang Gregorian Chant, smelled incense, and spoke Latin on the altar. But Jim also experienced the election of a new Pope, John XXIII, during high school and the excitement surrounding Vatican II during his years in college and graduate school. New questions were being asked; new instruments appeared at Mass (organs were out; guitars were in); new songs were being sung ("Kumbaya" instead of "Ave Maria"); new theologians were being read; new criticisms of the Church were being heard; new horizons were coming into view; a whole new Church was in the making.

Jim's Children: Post-Vatican II Catholics

After completing his Ph.D., Jim took a teaching position at Purdue University. While visiting the East Coast for Christmas in 1968, Jim met an Italian woman named Anna, who worked for Singer Company in New York. They married in 1971 and had two children, a boy (Jay) and a girl (Terry). Jim and Anna made sure their children knew all about their Irish and Italian ancestries. In the public grade schools and the public high school they attended, Jay and Terry met students from a wide variety of racial, ethnic, and religious backgrounds. Jay and Terry took on their parents' political preferences for the Democratic Party, but they grew up in an era when the political climate was dominated by Republican presidents Reagan and Bush. Their formative years have included the economic polarization of society in the 1980s (more millionaires and more homeless at the same time); scientific and technological disasters such as Three Mile Island, Chernobyl, and the Challenger; conflicts in the Middle East, Grenada, and Haiti; the women's movement; the decline of the Soviet Union; gay rights; drugs; AIDS; being told their generation would be the first not to do better than their parents' generation; and many divorces among their schoolmates' parents.

In their church, they've known a conservative Pope; declining numbers of priests and nuns; increased reliance on lay teachers in religious education classes (laymen and women have had much more to do with their religious formation than nuns have); reports of pedophilia among priests; growing up in a progressive campus ministry affiliated with Purdue; relationships with priests based on personality and friendship as much as on authority; less emphasis on understanding church history and traditions, and more on taking responsibility for their own "faith journeys"; and vigorous debates between highly committed Catholics over issues such as abortion and the ordination of priests. They and other Catholics in their generation have had far more frequent interaction with Protestants, Jews, persons of other faiths, and unchurched persons than their paternal grandmother and father had when they were growing up. Their high school boyfriends and girlfriends were Protestants, not Catholics. Jay is attending the University of Dayton, a Catholic college. Terry is a high school senior; she'll attend Indiana University when she graduates.

As this one extended family indicates, three generations of Catholics have experienced three very different worlds and three very different churches. Members of Louise's generation learned to love their country and their Church. They respect civil and religious authorities; they were taught to do what their elders asked them to do. The Church is a very important part of their lives; they believe in it and know they have to support it. They are most likely to emphasize church authority and the importance of participating in the Church.

Members of Jim's generation learned about stability and respect when they were young kids, but as they got to be teenagers and young adults, things changed. There were important challenges to civil authorities during the 1960s, and religious authorities in the wake of Vatican II. The Church was important, but many of its "eternal truths" were changing, and many good people (including talented young priests and nuns) were wondering whether to stay in or get out of the Church. This generation is most likely to have mixed feelings about authority (versus making up its own mind) and institutional commitment (versus personal spirituality).

Jim's children and others their age have learned that they can't always depend on others, whether civil authorities (they think of Watergate), scientists (of the Challenger explosion), employers (of numerous layoffs, sometimes of thousands), parents (of divorces), or religious authorities (of bishops having affairs with women, priests practicing pedophilia). They've also been taught to make up their own minds about a host of new issues (for example, how to define the roles of husband and wife; how much to emphasize work and family; whether abortions are moral; whether gay couples are entitled to job benefits the way heterosexual couples are; how much to help dying parents). They are least likely of all to depend on church authority and the most likely of all to think of their faith in personal, not institutional, terms.

The Generations: Social Profiles

What are the social characteristics of the three generations of Catholics? Our 1993 survey indicates what the members of each generation are like (see Table 4.1).

The "typical" pre-Vatican II Catholic (55 years of age or older) in our study is a white, married woman who lives in the East, went to Catholic grade school, and is a high school graduate. She is not part of the labor force and lives on an annual income of $30,000 or less. The "typical" Vatican II Catholic (35-54 years of age) is similar in

Table 4.1
Social Characteristics of Three Generations of Catholics

Characteristic	Pre-Vatican II (N=185)* (%)	Vatican II (N=313) (%)	Post-Vatican II (N=304) (%)
Sex			
Male	37	44	58
Female	62	56	42
Marital Status			
Married	56	67	41
Never married	4	8	49
Widowed, divorced, separated	40	26	8
Education			
High school or less	77	51	51
Some college or more	21	48	47
Catholic schooling			
Grade school	43	55	53
High school	19	28	24
College	7	10	8
Occupation			
White collar			
Owner, manager	3	14	9
Professional	6	23	16
Clerical, sales	7	21	18
Blue collar			
Skilled	9	12	13
Semi-skilled, unskilled	12	16	23
Other			
Full-time student	—	1	6
Homemaker	12	2	2
Retired	46	2	—
Other	1	3	6
Income			
Less than $10,000	24	11	17
$10,000-$29,000	36	32	47
$30,000-$49,000	16	32	22
$50,000 or more	9	31	9
No response	15	3	5

*N indicates the number of cases in each column.

many ways to her pre-Vatican II counterpart. She also is white and married and lives in the East. She too went to a Catholic grade school and graduated from high school. However, she is in the labor force, most likely in a white-collar occupation (professional or clerical and sales), with an income in the $30,000 to $49,999 range. The "typical" post-Vatican II Catholic (18-34 years of age) is a white, single male who lives in the East. He went to Catholic grade school and graduated from high school. He is in a white collar occupation and makes $10,000 to $29,999 a year.

Authority in the Church

How do the three generations look at the Church? To what extent do they have different views of authority and different patterns of involvement in the Church?

In Chapter 2, we quoted Max Weber (1947:324) who wrote that authority is "the probability that certain specific commands from a given source will be obeyed by a given group of persons." Prior to Vatican II, the Pope, bishops, priests, and nuns claimed authority in virtually all aspects of church life. Since Vatican II, however, there has been considerable debate over the extent and nature of the clergy's authority. Several options have been discussed. The most top-down option is for priests and nuns to have as much authority as they had prior to the Council, with laypeople continuing to think and act in the relatively obedient manner they did theretofore. A more democratic option is for clergy and laypeople to share responsibility equally for the development of policies and practices that reflect the values, interests, and experiences of all Catholics. This option has taken many forms ranging from a purely collaborative model to one that stresses a new division of labor that gives clergy special authority in areas such as theology, sacraments, and liturgy, and laypeople more authority in areas such as church administration and finance, sexual ethics, and economic and political matters in the community. The most bottom-up proposal is for laypeople to assume responsibility for their own faith (making up their own minds about what to believe and how to act as Catholics) and for clergy to serve as facilitators and professional resource persons carrying out the wishes of the Catholic community. Our study gave us an opportunity to see what different generations of Catholics think about such issues.

We asked Catholics whether their confidence in the Pope and bishops had increased, decreased, or remained about the same in the past five years. Overall, we are impressed with the relative stability in Catholics' views on this topic: a majority in all three generations reported relatively little change (see Table 4.2). At the same time, there were some perceptible generational differences. Members of the pre-Vatican II generation were most likely to say their confidence in the Pope and bishops had risen in recent years (18 percent for the Pope; 13 percent for bishops). Vatican II and post-Vatican II Catholics were most likely to say their confidence in bishops had declined (32 percent and 29 percent, respectively).

Table 4.2
Confidence among Three Generations of Catholics in Pope and Bishops over Past Five Years

Strength of Confidence	Pre-Vatican II (%)	Vatican II (%)	Post-Vatican II (%)
Pope			
No change	65	68	74
Less confident	16	17	15
More confident	18	14	10
Bishops			
No change	63	59	66
Less confident	23	32	29
More confident	13	8	3

When we asked Catholics a more concrete question about distribution of authority in the Church, we learned two things: a majority, regardless of generation, favored a more democratic Church, but Vatican II and post-Vatican II Catholics were more inclined than pre-Vatican II Catholics to prefer democracy at all levels of the Church (see Table 4.3). For example, 67 percent of post-Vatican II Catholics and 61 percent of Vatican II Catholics wanted more democracy at the parish level; 52 percent of pre-Vatican II Catholics felt that way.

Next we asked laypeople what they thought about the possibility of the laity's being more involved in formulating policies in areas such as parish finances, selecting parish priests, divorce and remarriage, birth control, and the ordination of women (see Table 4.4). Once again, there were major generational differences. In general, Vatican II and post-Vatican II Catholics approved lay participation more than pre-Vatican II Catholics did. For example, 83 percent of post-Vatican II Catholics and 75 percent of Vatican II Catholics think laypeople ought to be involved in selecting their priests, compared to 58 percent of

Table 4.3
Preference among Three Generations of Catholics for Democracy in the Church

Democracy at what level	Pre-Vatican II (%)	Vatican II (%)	Post-Vatican II (%)
Parish	52	61	67
Diocese	52	64	61
Vatican	54	57	61

pre-Vatican II Catholics. Sixty-six percent of Vatican II Catholics and 64 percent of post-Vatican II Catholics want more say regarding church teachings about divorce and remarriage, compared to 48 percent of people in the pre-Vatican II generation. Generational differences were smaller with regard to the parish budget, about which more than 80 percent in all generations wanted more say.

Table 4.4
Approval of Lay Participation in Church Decision-Making

Issue	Pre-Vatican II (%)	Vatican II (%)	Post-Vatican II (%)
How parish income is spent	81	82	84
Selection of priests	58	75	83
Ordaining women	53	60	69
Divorce	48	66	64
Birth control	53	67	63

We also asked Catholics who they feel should have the final say on important issues in the Church and in their lives: remarriage, birth control, abortion, homosexuality, and sex outside marriage. Respondents were given three choices: church leaders, individual Catholics, or both (leaders and the laity working together). The most common response on all five items was "individual Catholics." Again, there were significant generational differences, with post-Vatican II and Vatican II Catholics being most inclined to desire the final say on these issues, and pre-Vatican II Catholics being least inclined (see Table 4.5 and Figure 4.1). On all five of the items we examined, there was a trend across generations toward more emphasis on laypeople's reaching their own decisions.

Table 4.5
Belief among Three Generations of Catholics that Individuals Should have the Final Say on Moral Issues

Issue	Pre-Vatican II (%)	Vatican II (%)	Post-Vatican II (%)
Divorce and remarriage	31	38	42
Birth control	46	59	62
Abortion	36	42	50
Homosexuality	25	41	51
Sex out of marriage	34	42	51

Finally, we asked Catholics whether they thought ordaining women and married men was a good idea. In general, a majority of Catholics in all three generations approved of the ordination of married men (75 percent of post-Vatican II Catholics, 70 percent of Vatican II and pre-Vatican II Catholics). The generations were more sharply divided on the ordination of women: while 72 percent of post-Vatican II Catholics and 66 percent of Vatican II Catholics approved; only 48 percent of pre-Vatican II Catholics did.

Figure 4.1
Percent Saying Individuals Should Have Final Say on Moral Issues

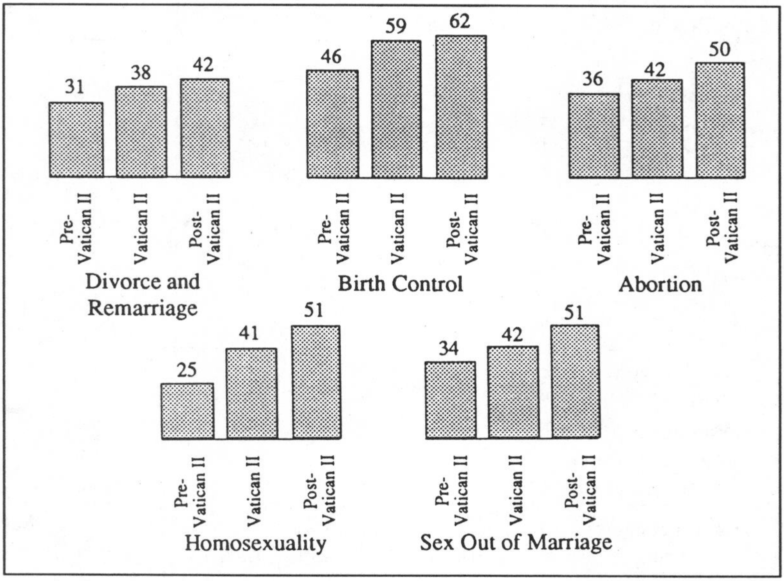

Religious Commitment

Religious commitment is both subjective and behavioral (D'Antonio *et al*, 1989). It encompasses the importance people attach to the Church (salience) and their behavioral involvement in it (participation). Do different generations of Catholics attach differing amounts of importance to the Church? Do they differ in the extent and nature of their behavioral involvement in the Church?

When we asked Catholics about the importance they attach to the Church, there were sharp generational differences (see Table 4.6 and Figure 4.2). Fifty-nine percent of pre-Vatican II Catholics said the Church is an important part of their lives; 48 percent of Vatican II Catholics and only 29 percent of post-Vatican II Catholics said so. Eighty-three percent of pre-Vatican II Catholics said they could never imagine leaving the Church, compared to 58 percent of Vatican II Catholics and 50 percent of post-Vatican II Catholics.

Table 4.6
Religious Commitment among Three Generations of Catholics

Commitment Aspect	Pre-Vatican II (%)	Vatican II (%)	Post-Vatican II (%)
Church is important	59	48	29
Would never leave the Catholic Church*	83	58	50
Attend Mass			
Once a week or more	63	45	24
Almost every week	10	16	17
About once a month	9	18	22
Less than once a month	18	21	36
Pray			
Daily	90	67	53
Weekly, occasionally	6	25	30
Seldom, never	3	7	15
Know of pastoral letter on			
Women	60	51	29
Economic justice	26	24	11
Peace	24	21	12

*These percentages represent points 1 and 2 on the 7 point scale, with point 1 being "I would never leave the Catholic Church."

Figure 4.2
Measures of Religious Commitment (Percents)

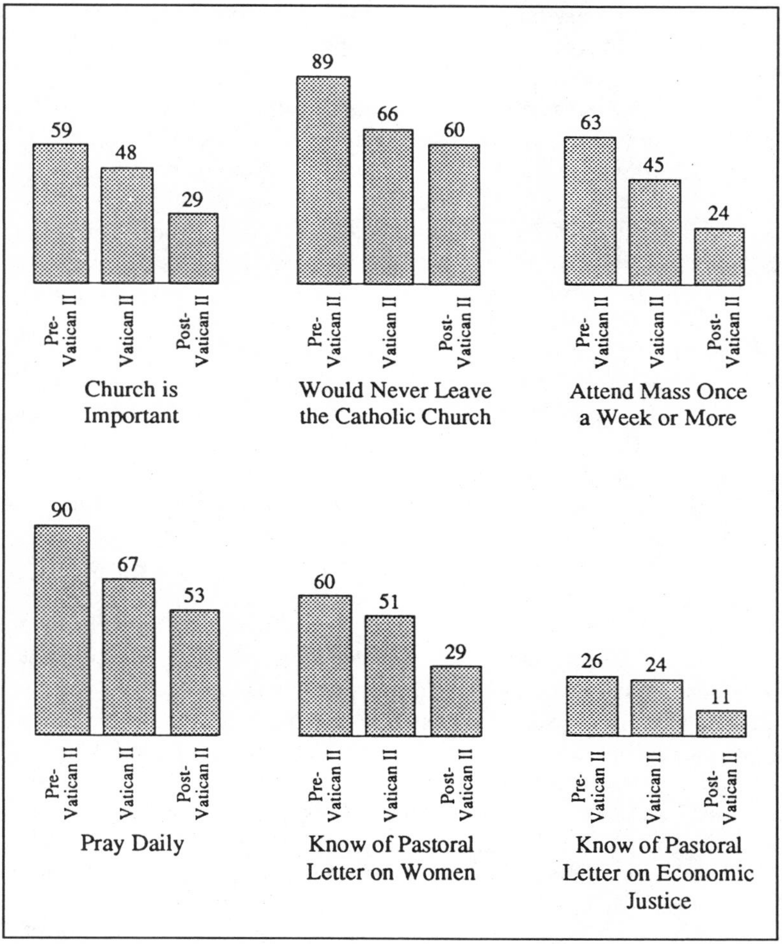

Turning to actual behaviors, we asked how often our respondents attend Mass. Pre-Vatican II Catholics reported attending far more regularly than younger generations of Catholics; 63 percent attended at least weekly. Only 45 percent of Vatican II Catholics and only 24 percent of post-Vatican II Catholics attended that frequently. Conversely, more than a third of young Catholics attended less than once a month, but only 18 percent of pre-Vatican Catholics were that inactive.

There also is a decline in the frequency of prayer across generational lines. Ninety percent of pre-Vatican II Catholics, 67 percent of Vatican II Catholics, and only 53 percent of post-Vatican II Catholics said they pray daily. About five times as many young Catholics as older Catholics (15 percent vs. 3 percent) said they seldom or never pray.

Another of our survey questions concerned the American bishops' pastoral letters on the role of women in the Church (1992), economic justice (1986), and peace (1983). In general, more of the respondents had heard of the pastoral letter on the role of women (44 percent) than had heard of either of the other two letters (19 percent and 18 percent, respectively). However, there also were large generational differences. Pre-Vatican II Catholics were two to three times more likely than post-Vatican II Catholics to have heard of all three letters.

Next, we asked people about their concept of being a "good Catholic" (see table 4.7). Specifically, whether one can be a good Catholic without engaging in a variety of behaviors that have long been a part of the Catholic tradition (e.g., without attending Mass weekly, without donating time or money to one's parish). Once again, pre-Vatican II Catholics had the most institutional sense of being Catholic and post-Vatican II Catholics the least. Sixty percent of the older cohort said one can be a good Catholic without going to Mass weekly, while 74 percent of Vatican II Catholics and 80 percent of post-Vatican II Catholics thought so.

Another illustration of the younger generation's deinstitutionalized sense of being Catholic was its greater tendency to say one can be a good Catholic without obeying church teachings on birth control, abortion, and divorce and remarriage. This pattern occurred across generations on six of the nine items in Table 4.7. On another item, the Vatican II and post-Vatican II generations were most likely to say one can be a good Catholic without marrying in the Church. The Vatican II generation was least likely to say one can be a good Catholic without donating time or money to help the poor and the parish.

When we asked respondents whether their commitment to the Church had increased, decreased, or remained about the same during the past five years, generational differences appeared once again (see Table 4.8). Post-Vatican II Catholics were about twice as likely as pre-Vatican II Catholics to say they were less committed than they were five years ago. The oldest generation of Catholics was more steadfast in its commitment.

When we asked how particular church teachings and recent developments had affected our respondents' commitment, we learned that

Table 4.7
Belief among Three Generations of Catholics That You Can Be a Good Catholic

Personal Religious Practice	Pre-Vatican II (%)	Vatican II (%)	Post-Vatican II (%)
Without donating to Peter's Pence	72	80	83
Without observing church strictures against birth control	59	73	82
Without going to Mass weekly	60	74	80
Without observing church strictures against divorce and remarriage	50	64	67
Without observing church strictures against abortion	40	53	67
Without marrying in the Church	53	65	64
Without donating to the parish	55	51	63
Without helping the poor	57	41	58
Without believing in infallibility	42	51	55

commitment transcended specific issues (see Table 4.9). The most common response was "no effect." However, when there was an effect, it followed generational lines. Pre-Vatican II Catholics were most likely to say that teachings on such matters as birth control, abortion, and the ordination of women had strengthened their faith. Vatican II and post-Vatican II Catholics were most inclined to say such teachings had weakened their commitment. Recent reports of homosexuality and pedophilia among Catholic priests, while disturbing to many Catholics, bothered older Catholics the least and younger Catholics the most.

Table 4.8
Church Commitment among Three Generations of Catholics over Past Five Years

Strength of Commitment	Pre-Vatican II (%)	Vatican II (%)	Post-Vatican II (%)
No change	60	49	44
Less committed	17	21	33
More committed	19	26	20

Table 4.9
Effects of Church Teachings and Recent Developments on Religious Commitment among Three Generations of Catholics

	Pre-Vatican II (%)	Vatican II (%)	Post-Vatican II (%)
Birth control			
No effect	65	48	42
Weakened	15	36	42
Strengthened	15	13	9
Abortion			
No effect	40	37	33
Weakened	12	23	28
Strengthened	45	35	35
Not ordaining women			
No effect	59	52	58
Weakened	14	31	27
Strengthened	21	14	11
Homosexuality among priests			
No effect	59	57	50
Weakened	29	34	39
Strengthened	4	2	6
Pedophilia among priests			
No effect	53	42	34
Weakened	35	51	58
Strengthened	3	3	4

Conclusions

There are three quite distinct generations of laypeople in the Church today: pre-Vatican II, Vatican II, and post-Vatican II Catholics. Each generation has experienced a very different world and a very different religious upbringing. Louise's upbringing included a rather static, hierarchical Church in which institutional commitment was the norm. Her son Jim and his generation learned the importance of the Church, but also learned that it can change, especially its norms of authority (more democratic) and commitment (more voluntary). Jim's children and others in their generation learned that the Church is "the people of God" and that laypeople ought to be involved in virtually all aspects of church life.

As a result of their dissimilar experiences, the three generations have different views of authority. Pre-Vatican II Catholics tend to prefer the hierarchical model of Church with which they became familiar during their formative years. Post-Vatican II Catholics prefer the democratic model to which they were exposed. Pre-Vatican II Catholics also exhibit higher levels of institutional commitment in terms of public practices such as Mass attendance and supporting the Church financially; they report as well more frequent devotional activity, such as private prayer. Post-Vatican II Catholics have the least institutional sense of what it means to be Catholic; they attend Mass less regularly, don't feel as great an obligation to support the Church as a social institution, and are less devotionally active. Vatican II Catholics tend to fall between these two extremes, although they are a bit more like the post-Vatican II generation than the pre-Vatican II generation.

The generational differences account for a great deal of the pluralism in the Church today. The generations experience the Church in different ways, have very different feelings about the Church and their personal spirituality, and express these feelings in very dissimilar terms. They are responsible for many of the most vigorous debates in the Church today.

As time passes, the American Catholic laity will move inexorably from belief in hierarchy to belief in democracy, and from high levels of institutional commitment to emphasis on individual commitment. These trends will put increased pressure on church leaders to move in like directions or risk further alienation and/or defection among post-Vatican II Catholics. Whether the institutional Church will move in these directions remains to be seen.

References

D'Antonio, William V., James D. Davidson, Dean R. Hoge, and Ruth Wallace. 1989. *American Catholic Laity in a Changing Church.* Kansas City, MO: Sheed & Ward.

Davidson, James D., and Andrea S. Williams. 1993. "Generations of Catholics: Results of Focus Groups." Paper presented at the annual meeting of the Association for the Sociology of Religion, Miami.

Hoge, Dean R., Benton Johnson, and Donald Luidens. 1994. *Vanishing Boundaries.* Louisville: Westminister/John Knox Press.

Kennedy, Eugene. 1990. *Tomorrow's Catholics, Yesterday's Church*, New York: Harper & Row.

McNamara, Patrick, 1993. *Conscience First, Tradition Second.* Albany, NY: SUNY Press.

Mannheim, Karl. 1952. *Essays on the Sociology of Knowledge.* New York: Oxford University Press.

Roof, Wade Clark. 1993. *A Generation of Seekers.* San Francisco: Harper.

Walrath, Douglas. 1987. *Frameworks.* New York: Pilgrim Press.

Weber, Max. 1947. *The Theory of Social and Economic Organization.* Glencoe, IL: Free Press.

Williams, Andrea S., and James D. Davidson. 1994. "Catechism Catholics, Council Catholics, and Christian Catholics: A Theory of Catholic Generations." Paper presented at the annual meeting of the Religious Research Association, Albuquerque. November.

5

Post-Vatican II Catholics: Central Tendencies and Intra-Generational Differences

WHEN ONE OF THE AUTHORS MET WITH TWO BISHOPS TO DISCUSS A study he was initiating in their dioceses, he asked the bishops what they wanted to learn the most. Both gave the same answer: "Tell us what young Catholics are like." The bishops explained that their daily schedules keep them in regular contact with middle-aged and older Catholics, whom they feel they understand pretty well, but that they have much less contact with young Catholics and don't understand them as well.

We hope this chapter helps all clergy and lay leaders who want to know more about Catholics who have been raised in the post-Vatican II Church. We first describe the religious beliefs and practices of Catholics under 35 years of age. We focus then on differences within that cohort. Two factors produce the most consistent differences: sex and amount of Catholic schooling. Young Catholic males are very different from young Catholic females, and young Catholics with extensive Catholic schooling are quite different from others in the cohort who have had lesser amounts of Catholic education.

Central Tendencies

Several recent studies suggest a religious profile of young Catholics who have been raised entirely in the post-Vatican II Church. In addition to our own 1987 and 1993 surveys, these studies include McNamara's (1993) longitudinal study of students attending a Catholic high school in New Mexico, D'Antonio's (1994) analysis of data from a 1993 survey commissioned by Catholics for a Free Choice (CFFC), and focus groups that Davidson and Williams have conducted with young Catholics in Indiana (Davidson and Williams, 1993; Williams and Davidson, 1994). Our review of the studies yields eight central tendencies.

• Post-Vatican II Catholics *place a higher priority on being good Christians than they do on being good Catholics*. Reversing the pre-Vatican II Church's emphasis on being "the one true Church" and differentiating itself from other Christian faiths, the post-Vatican II Church has stressed a more ecumenical emphasis on what Catholicism has in common with other Christian faith groups. This emphasis has been an integral part of young Catholics' religious education (McNamara, 1993). Hence, post-Vatican II Catholics are more inclined to think of themselves as Christians who happen to be Catholic than as Catholics who are fundamentally different from other Christians (the pre-Vatican II emphasis).

This tendency is evident in Davidson and Williams' recent focus groups with post-Vatican II Catholics. When the two researchers asked what it takes to be a "good Catholic," the young Catholics often redefined the issue, preferring to talk about what it takes to be a "good Christian." Here's what three of them told Davidson and Williams.

> It's not so important that a person be a good Catholic; it's more important to me that a person be a good Christian.
>
> Be a good Christian; denomination doesn't have anything to do with it.
>
> I'd rather be a Christian than a good Catholic.

• Older generations tend to give great weight to the institutional nature of the Church. They single out its teaching authority, the holiness of priests and sisters, the extent to which being Catholic is an ascriptive quality tied to one's ancestry, the laity's need to comply with church teachings, the importance of the sacraments, and the importance of protecting and perpetuating the Church.

Post-Vatican II Catholics think differently. *They tend to have a deinstitutionalized and democratic view of the Church*. They are more inclined to think of the Church as "the people of God." They stress the volitional aspects of being in the Church – the need to make a personal decision to be Catholic, and the individual's need to choose his or her own religious beliefs and lifestyle.

Kennedy (1990:18-19) highlighted the difference between "Culture One" (usually older) Catholics' institutional view of the Church and "Culture Two" (usually younger) Catholics' tendency to see Catholicism "as a way of life." In Kennedy's (1990:21) words:

> Culture Two Catholics are often too busy to notice what is playing at the long-running institutional festival. . . . They observe it, respect its leaders and official members, but they are not emotionally involved with or imaginatively dominated by it. . . . They form their own consciences as they confront multiple daily choices; they exhibit a readiness to do this without necessarily perceiving themselves as rebels against the institutional order of the first culture.

Many of the young Catholics McNamara (1993:104-105) interviewed expressed this individualized view of the Church:

> I think the Church's job is to make sure we are all well informed. Its opinion carries a lot of weight, but in the end we have to choose for ourselves the way we want to live.
>
> I think that religion is a private thing between the individual and God and that the Church only serves as a guide to help when things seem unclear.
>
> I really don't believe that any religious group has the right to tell people how to run their lives. They are there to offer advice and set guidelines. God gave us free will in order to choose for ourselves.

Young Catholics in our 1987 and 1993 surveys revealed the same pattern, as did Davidson and Williams' focus groups. D'Antonio's analysis of the 1993 CFFC survey yields a similar picture.

• Post-Vatican II Catholics *make a rather sharp distinction between God's law and Church law and, when the two are in tension with each other, put higher priority on God's law than on Church law.* Pre-Vatican II Catholics assume that God's law and Church law are one and the same thing. When God speaks, it is through the Church; when the Church speaks, it is God speaking. Post-Vatican II Catholics think otherwise: God loves them; they have direct access to the Creator's love; and the Church is a human institution that tries to interpret God's love but often is too rigid and legalistic. When forced to choose, post-Vatican II Catholics prefer to follow God's law.

One of the people in the Davidson and Williams' focus groups reflected young Catholics' tendency to emphasize God's law when she said: "[My faith] is very personal. It's between me and God and no one else." Another said: "When I die I have to answer to God, not to

Father So-and-So, not to the pope." Another said: "The pope is just an elected official." Another put it even more harshly:

> Quite honestly, I have a real hard time aligning myself with a bunch of out of touch, prejudiced, racist old men that are priests and that are leaders of the Church. I see a bunch of Irish Catholic bishops and archbishops – and that's what I am, Irish – and I'm lookin' and goin' "you're not what I'm about." . . . I have a real difficult time accepting these people who . . . don't practice what they preach.

• Post-Vatican II Catholics are more likely than older Catholics *to disagree with specific Church teachings.* Our 1987 study showed that post-Vatican II Catholics were the most likely to say that individual laypersons, not Church authorities, should have final say on a variety of issues related to faith and morals. Our 1993 survey revealed the same pattern: young Catholics are most inclined to question beliefs on such matters as papal infallibility, birth control, and abortion, and least likely to accept behavioral standards such as regular attendance at Mass. McNamara (1993) reported that young Catholics tend to be very selective in their beliefs, agreeing with some more than others. The vast majority of young Catholics in the CFFC 1993 survey believed it "possible to disagree with church teaching and still be a good Catholic" (D'Antonio, 1994). One of the young Catholics in the focus groups summed it up very well: "I'm comfortable being a Catholic, but I have my own mind and I don't believe in everything the Catholic church does."

• Post-Vatican II Catholics *view God as an all-loving and forgiving friend who wants us to be nice to others.* Describing his post-Vatican II upbringing, Markey (1994:19) said:

> Our catechism and theology emphasized the love and goodness of God. God was not portrayed as a punishing, vengeful father, nor as a distant, cold and heartless judge. God was always the compassionate and tender parent who only wanted the best for the children.

Markey argues that this image of God has fostered a nihilistic sense of not being able to work to any effect against evil (for example poverty, hunger, oppression). As a result, post-Vatican II Catholics have been raised on what he calls the " 'theology of being nice': God is nice, so we should all be nice too and try not to worry too much, because there is basically nothing you can do about it [evil] anyway" (Markey, 1994:20).

This orientation was very apparent in the Davidson and Williams focus groups: post-Vatican II Catholics emphasized the importance of "being a nice person." Reflecting on their experiences in religious education, two of their numbers said:

> In CCD classes we just talked about being nice to each other; it wasn't a real dogmatic approach . . . more of a general Christian approach.
>
> [We were] taught to be nice to each other.

• Post-Vatican II Catholics *are relatively uninformed about Church teachings*. Our 1987 survey showed that young Catholics are less likely than older Catholics to have heard of the American bishops' pastoral letters on peace (1983) and economic justice (1986). Our 1993 survey revealed the same pattern: only 11 percent of post-Vatican II Catholics said they had heard of the economic pastoral, only 12 percent reported knowing anything about the peace pastoral, and only 29 percent had heard of the bishops' recent attempt to write a pastoral on the status of women in the Church. In each case, older Catholics were two to three times more likely to say they knew about these pastoral letters.

Post-Vatican II Catholics are aware that they are less informed than older generations of Catholics, and Davidson and Williams were told as much:

> I don't think that I was really taught to understand why we believe what we believe. It was more like you were told "this is what you should believe." But why?
>
> As far as the Bible goes, I couldn't even tell you what's in the Old and New Testaments.
>
> I don't know what it means to be a good Catholic.
>
> I haven't found out why being Catholic is any better than being Methodist.

Moreover, they feel shortchanged by the Church. They say their religious education did not emphasize the substance of their faith. Listen to how they describe their experiences:

> I'm appalled by what I was [not] taught in CCD.
>
> I didn't know what parts of the Mass mean. They didn't really tell us.
>
> We just shot paper wads in religion class.

In the absence of religious grounding post-Vatican II Catholics feel vulnerable. Because their social experiences are so much more ecumenical than their parents' and grandparents', they are more likely to be asked questions by Protestants and members of other faiths. They are embarrassed when they don't have answers. With sadness in her voice, one young Catholic told Davidson and Williams: "I wish they had a little book so I can look up Pentecost and see what it is."

• Post-Vatican II Catholics *lack a vocabulary to help them form a Catholic identity and interpret their Catholic experiences.* Davidson and Williams found that older generations of Catholics have a vocabulary rich in specifically Catholic words. They talk about things like mortal sin, venial sin, original sin, the Blessed Virgin Mary, the Baltimore Catechism, retreats, Stations of the Cross, Holy Days of Obligation, confession, rosary beads, and not eating meat on Friday. Listening to them, one knows they are Catholic and that they have a common language with which to communicate with one another about their Catholic experiences.

Post-Vatican II Catholics have not acquired a Catholic word bank upon which to draw. They use fewer specifically Catholic words and tend to talk in generic Christian terms. Except for their occasional references to RCIA or RENEW, one wouldn't know whether they are Catholics or members of any mainline Protestant denomination.

• Older generations of Catholics learned that some behaviors are naturally right and others are naturally wrong according to God's plan. Pre-marital sex is wrong because sex is for procreative purposes and is to take place in marriage, not before. Abortion is against God's law because it involves taking a life. Homosexuality is wrong because it is not natural. Divorce and remarriage are wrong because God wants people to stay together for a lifetime.

Post-Vatican II Catholics have learned that *the rightness or wrongness of one's actions depend on the circumstance and the effects such actions have on others.* To determine what is right or wrong, one must weigh the costs and benefits of one's actions. When the benefits outweigh the costs, the actions are probably right; when the costs outweigh the benefits, they probably are not. Thus, pre-marital sex may be right if it reaffirms the commitment between two persons who intend to get married. Abortion may be right if the costs of having an unwanted child exceed the benefits. Homosexual actions may be right if they take place in the context of a meaningful, long-term relationship between two genetically determined gays or lesbians. Divorce may be right if the marriage is doing more harm than good to both partners.

The Davidson and Williams focus groups revealed how extensive this "consequentialist" approach to morality and ethics is among post-Vatican II Catholics. Here's what two young Catholics said:

> When making your decision, you have to decide if someone is going to get hurt.
>
> If you're going to do anything [pre-marital sex], be prepared for the consequences, and you also have a responsibility toward God; if your conscience lets you get away with it and your spirituality doesn't suffer, fine.

Intra-Generational Differences

Of course, post-Vatican II Catholics aren't all alike. As we showed in the previous chapter, there are many social differences among young Catholics. They also do not think and act in lock step with regard to religious matters. They have widely variant concepts of authority, and the extent and nature of their involvement in the Church is far from uniform. In this section we examine the relationship between the social and religious differences among post-Vatican II Catholics.

Of all the social characteristics included in our study, the one that most systematically differentiated among post-Vatican II Catholics' religious orientations was sex. Young male and young female Catholics think and act very differently. Specifically, post-Vatican II women are more oriented toward democracy in the Church than young Catholic men are. They also are more highly committed, yet more alienated, than post-Vatican II men.

Sex Differences

When we asked post-Vatican II Catholics whether there should be more democracy at the Vatican, diocesan, and parish levels of the Church, women were consistently more inclined than men to say yes. The largest gap appeared at the diocesan level, where 73 percent of women favored more democracy, compared with only 53 percent of men, but the gaps were significant at the parish and Vatican levels as well (see Table 5.1).

Women also were more predisposed to participating in decisions at all levels of Church life (see Table 5.2 and Figure 5.1). Fully 81 percent of women, compared to 61 percent of men, said that laypeople ought to be involved in any discussions about ordaining women. Women also were more likely to say that laypeople ought to be involved in policy decisions related to divorce and remarriage (75 percent) and

Table 5.1
Preference among Post-Vatican II Catholics for Democracy in the Church

Democracy at what level	Males (%)	Females (%)	Difference (%)
Parish	58	79	21
Diocesean	53	71	18
Vatican	57	66	9

Table 5.2
Approval among Post-Vatican II Catholics of Lay Participation in Church Decision-Making

Issue	Males (%)	Females (%)	Difference (%)
Ordaining women	61	81	20
Divorce	56	75	19
Birth control	58	71	13
How parish income is spent	81	89	8
Selecting parish priests	80	88	8

Figure 5.1
Post-Vatican II Catholics:
Percent Approving Lay Participation in Decision-Making

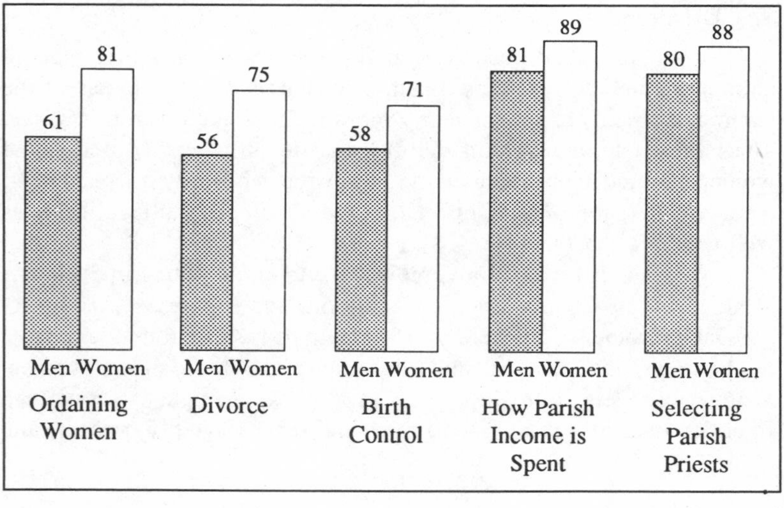

to birth control (71 percent). Women more than men also felt that laypeople ought to participate in decisions regarding parish finances and the selection of parish priests, though the sex differences on these two items were smaller.

When asked who should have the final say on a number of important issues, women were more inclined than men were to grant ultimate authority to individual Catholics, not church officials (see Table 5.3). Sex differences were largest on three issues: birth control, sex outside marriage, and homosexuality. Differences were smaller, though in the same direction, on two other issues: abortion, and divorce and remarriage.

Table 5.3
Belief among Post-Vatican II Catholics that Individuals Should Have a Say on Moral Issues

Issue	Males (%)	Females (%)	Difference (%)
Birth control	58	68	10
Sex out of marriage	47	57	10
Homosexuality	42	52	10
Abortion	49	53	4
Divorce and remarriage	41	43	2

By and large, post-Vatican II women are also more religious than young Catholic males (see Table 5.4). Women were more likely to say that the Church is an important part of their lives (35 percent). They also reported attending Mass on a more regular basis (32 percent at least weekly versus 19 percent for males), praying more often (66 percent daily), and being more aware of recent pastoral letters on the role of women in the Church, economic justice, and peace. The only item on which men seemed more committed than women concerned the possibility of leaving the Church. Fifty-four percent of post-Vatican II men, compared to only 46 percent of women, said they could not imagine any circumstances under which they might leave. In later sections of this chapter, we point to some of the reasons that women's commitment is more conditional than men's.

Despite their relatively high levels of religious commitment, young Catholic women are less traditional than men on many issues (see Table 5.5). For example, 73 percent of women, compared with only 57 percent of men, said one can be a good Catholic without

Table 5.4
Religious Commitment among Post-Vatican II Catholics

Commitment Aspect	Males (%)	Females (%)	Difference (%)
Church is one the most important parts of my life	25	35	10
I would never leave the Catholic Church (1-2 on 7 point scale)	54	46	-8
Attend Mass			
Once a week or more	19	32	13
Almost every week	16	18	2
About once a month	25	20	-5
Less than once a month	38	30	-8
Pray			
Daily	43	66	23
Weekly, occasionally	33	27	-6
Seldom, never	21	7	-14
Know of pastoral letters on			
Women	27	32	7
Economic justice	9	12	3
Peace	11	14	3

marrying in the Church. Seventy-six percent of women, but only 61 percent of men, said it is possible to be a good Catholic without agreeing with the Church's views on abortion. Sizable sex differences also appeared in men's and women's views on the importance of obeying the Church's proscription of divorce and remarriage, on the importance of attending Mass weekly, on the Church's stand against birth control, and on its doctrine of papal infallibility. There were no appreciable differences between the sexes on three other issues: contributing to Peter's Pence, donating to the parish, and helping the poor.

When we asked post-Vatican II Catholics whether their commitment to their local parishes had changed during the past five years, men and women gave us different answers (see Table 5.6). Men tended to say their commitment had not changed (51 percent); women were more likely to say their commitment had declined (38 percent).

Which church teachings or events have most affected men's and women's commitment to the Church? (see Table 5.7). Sex differences were greatest regarding the effects of the Church's birth control teaching. Women were more likely than men (53 percent versus 35 percent)

Table 5.5
Among Post-Vatican II Catholics Belief that One Can Be a Good Catholic in the Absence of Certain Religious Practices

Personal Religious Practice	Males (%)	Females (%)	Difference (%)
Largest male-female differences			
Without marrying in the Church	57	73	16
Without Church teaching on abortion	61	76	15
Without Church teaching on divorce and remarriage	63	73	10
Without going to Mass weekly	83	75	-8
Without Church teaching on birth control	78	86	8
Without believing in infallibility	52	60	8
Smallest male-female differences			
Without donating to Peter's Pence	83	82	-1
Without donating to the parish	64	61	-3
Without helping the poor	59	57	-2

to say this teaching had weakened their commitment. There also were important sex differences with regard to abortion. Women were more likely to say the Church's views on abortion had weakened their commitment (39 percent). Men were more inclined to say the Church's abortion teaching had *increased* their commitment (39 percent); 36 percent said that it had not affected their commitment. In striking contrast to women their age, only 20 percent of young men said it had weakened their faith.

Sex differences also appeared in the data on homosexuality among priests. Women were more inclined than men to say reports of such behavior had no effect on their commitment (58 percent versus 44

Table 5.6
Religious Commitment among Post-Vatican II Catholics over the Past Five Years

Strength of Commitment	Males (%)	Females (%)	Difference (%)
No change	51	35	-16
Less committed	30	38	8
More committed	18	22	4

Table 5.7
Effects of Church Teachings and Recent Developments on Post-Vatican II Catholics' Religious Commitment

	Males (%)	Females (%)	Difference (%)
Birth control			
No effect	48	33	-15
Weakened	35	53	18
Strengthened	8	10	2
Abortion			
No effect	36	30	-6
Weakened	20	39	19
Strengthened	39	30	-9
Not ordaining women			
No effect	57	59	2
Weakened	25	31	6
Strengthened	14	7	-7
Homosexuality among priests			
No effect	44	58	14
Weakened	42	36	-6
Strengthened	9	1	-8
Pedophilia among priests			
No effect	35	32	-3
Weakened	57	60	3
Strengthened	5	3	-2

percent). There were no appreciable sex differences on the items having to do with the ordination of women and reports of pedophilia among priests. Both sexes were more disturbed by reports of pedophilia than any other issue we considered.

To recap, post-Vatican II women are less traditional than men with regard to authority. Women, more than men, believe that laypeople ought to be participating in a wide range of decisions, especially those that affect their parishes and their personal lives. Post-Vatican II women also are more religious than their male counterparts, yet are less traditional in their conception of what it means to be Catholic and are more likely to report feeling more distance between themselves and the Church as a result of sex-related issues such as birth control and abortion. Separate analyses not shown here indicate that overall these sex differences are larger among post-Vatican II Catholics than they are among older generations of Catholics.

Catholic Education

Amount of Catholic schooling also has important effects on young Catholics' religious beliefs and practices (see Table 5.8). We put young Catholics into one of four categories according to levels of Catholic schooling they had had: none (44 percent), one (32 percent), two (19 percent), or all three (5 percent). In general, the differences between Catholics with no Catholic education, one level, or two levels were small and inconsistent. However, those with three levels of Catholic schooling (grade school, high school, and college) are markedly different. Young Catholics with the most Catholic schooling have high levels of religious commitment yet the least traditional views of authority in the Church.

Post-Vatican II Catholics with all three levels of Catholic schooling were two to three times more likely than their peers with less Catholic education to say their confidence in the Vatican had grown in the past five years. They also were five times more likely to say that their confidence in the American bishops had grown. However, they also were significantly more inclined to favor democracy at all levels of church life (suggesting that their desire for involvement in Church policies and programs is *not* linked to disenchantment with clerical leadership). For example, 80 percent favored more democracy at the Vatican level, 76 percent at the diocesan level, and 75 percent at the parish level.

Post-Vatican II Catholics with all three levels of education were more likely too, to stress the need for lay participation in decisions concerning divorce (83 percent), the ordination of women (82 percent), and birth control (81 percent). They were no different from others in their preference for lay involvement in parish financial matters. In the only real reversal of this pattern, post-Vatican II Catholics with all three levels of Catholic schooling were less inclined to favor lay participation in selecting parish priests (70 percent, compared with more than 80 percent of Catholics with less Catholic schooling).

When asked who should have final say on major issues, post-Vatican II Catholics with the most Catholic education were more likely than others to say individual Catholics. Eighty-two percent said individuals should have the final say on birth control practices; 65 percent,

Table 5.8
Effects of Catholic Education on Post-Vatican II Catholics' Concepts of Authority and Religious Commitment

	Catholic Education Level			
	None	One	Two	Three
Authority				
Confidence in Vatican				
No change	73	79	72	60
Less confident	19	13	12	17
More confident	8	8	12	23
Prefer Democracy in				
Parish	64	68	68	75
Diocese	55	61	68	76
Vatican	61	60	56	80
Laity should participate in decision-making				
Birth control	60	63	66	81
Selecting priests	81	85	88	70
Ordaining women	72	65	68	82
Individual should have final say regarding				
Birth control	60	61	65	82
Abortion	45	56	55	45
Divorce	42	39	40	63
Commitment				
Church is important	27	26	38	45
Attend Mass weekly	24	24	20	40
Know pastoral letter on peace	8	15	8	49
Can be good Catholic without:				
Marrying in the Church	55	68	72	79
Obeying Church teaching on abortion	68	67	70	59
Attending Mass weekly	79	79	80	87
Donating to parish	58	65	66	76
Commitment to Church in past five years				
No change	48	49	30	33
More	21	11	24	53
Less	27	39	44	5

(continued from previous page)	Catholic Education Level None	One	Two	Three
Effects on commitment				
Abortion				
No effect	35	32	34	20
Weakened	25	30	29	28
Strengthened	33	35	36	52
Not ordaining women				
No effect	62	60	51	35
Weakened	24	25	36	45
Strengthened	9	12	12	19
Birth control				
No effect	46	41	35	43
Weakened	35	48	51	34
Strengthened	10	9	3	23

on having sex outside marriage; and 83 percent, on getting divorced and on practicing homosexuality. Only when it came to having abortions did this group think differently. On the abortion issue, those with the most Catholic schooling were less inclined to give final authority to individuals (45 percent).

Compared with others in the same generation, post-Vatican II Catholics with all three levels of Catholic schooling exhibited high levels of religious commitment. They were significantly more likely to say the Church is an important part of their lives (45 percent), and that they were aware of recent pastoral letters on women in the Church (51 percent), peace (49 percent), and economic justice (30 percent). They were similar to other post-Vatican II Catholics in the frequency with which they prayed (54 percent daily).

When asked whether one can be a good Catholic without complying with traditional church norms, post-Vatican II Catholics with the most Catholic schooling were less traditional than others in the generation. They were more likely than peers with less Catholic schooling to say one can be a good Catholic without acting in accordance with the Church's view of birth control (96 percent), without contributing to Peter's Pence (91 percent), without attending Mass weekly (87 percent), without believing in infallibility (86 percent), without agreeing with church teachings on divorce and remarriage (86 percent), without marrying in the Church (79 percent), and without donating to the parish (76 percent). Their attitudes about donating to help the poor were no different from others (54 percent saying that doing so is not necessary to be a good Catholic). The only area where those with a great deal of Catholic schooling were more traditional than other post-Vatican II Catholics concerned abortion, where only 59 percent said one can be a good Catholic without obeying Church teachings.

Conclusions

Catholics raised entirely in the post-Vatican II Church are different in many ways from members of the pre-Vatican II and Vatican II generations discussed in the previous chapter. They are more inclined to think of themselves as Christians; to have a deinstitutionalized and democratic sense of "Church"; to distinguish between God's law and church law, and to attach higher priority to the former than the latter; to belong to the Church yet disagree with specific teachings; to think of God as a loving friend who wants us to be "nice persons"; to be uninformed about church teachings and to hold the Church (especially religious education programs) accountable for that circumstance; to lack a specifically-Catholic vocabulary with which to interpret their religious experiences; and to judge good and evil in terms of costs and benefits rather than principles of natural law. Some of these tendencies first appeared in recent studies of baby-boom Catholics (Fee *et al*, 1981; Roof, 1993); most have become evident in the more recent studies of the post-baby-boom generation we reviewed in this chapter.

Our results have important implications for the future. As older generations of Catholics die and are replaced by young Catholics, two things are likely to happen. As Greeley (1989) has noted, young Catholics are likely to become somewhat more involved and a bit more traditional as they pass through later stages of the life cycle. For example, when they get married and have children, they are likely to become somewhat more active in the Church and rely a bit more on religious authorities for guidance. The likelihood of this "rebound" or life-cycle effect checks any tendency toward overly dramatic projections that the future is going to be different from the past. Post-Vatican II Catholics will become a bit more like older Catholics in the years ahead.

However, as we argued in the previous chapter, many of the things young Catholics have experienced during their formative years will last throughout their lives. Post-Vatican II Catholics have been reared by parents and religious educators in ways that are very different from the past and that are likely to affect their orientations toward the

Church forever. For example, the Church's post-Vatican II emphases on having a Christian identity and being "the people of God" (rather than the one true hierachical Church) will have long-lasting effects on young Catholics' orientations toward the Church. So will young Catholics' deinstitutionalized and democratic view of the Church, their concept of a loving God, their tendency to distinguish between God's law and church law, and their consequentialist approach to morality.

We respond more positively to some of the likely trends than we do to others. We think church officials and religious educators should be praised for fostering a more general sense of being Christian among young Catholics, for encouraging young Catholics to take responsibility for their own religious orientations, for fostering the concept of a loving God, and for urging young Catholics to think about the consequences of their actions for others. These developments will have many beneficial effects in the years ahead. At the same time, we are concerned that young Catholics have little sense of what is special about being a Catholic Christian, lack a specifically Catholic vocabulary, and feel uninformed about their faith. These developments are likely to stifle individual commitment and Catholic solidarity in the years ahead. We think clergy and laypersons wanting to foster commitment and perpetuate a Catholic community ought to explore new ways of cultivating a Catholic identity, a specifically Catholic language, and a greater understanding of the Catholic tradition.

Young women are more committed yet less traditional than young men. Compared to men their age, they have less hierarchical conceptions of authority in the Church and put more emphasis on the importance of lay participation in most facets of church life, especially matters affecting their parishes or their personal lives. Their behaviors indicate they are more highly committed to the Church, yet they feel less committed than five years ago. This sense of alienation seems tied to the gap between their views on birth control and abortion and the views expressed by Church leaders. Separate analyses not reported in this chapter indicate that these sex differences are larger among post-Vatican II Catholics than among Vatican II and pre-Vatican II Catholics.

Post-Vatican II Catholics with the most Catholic schooling also are more committed yet less traditional than young Catholics with less Catholic schooling. They are more in favor of democracy and lay participation in virtually all aspects of church life except in selecting parish priests. Although they are more highly active in the Church than others their age, they also are more individualistic in their decision making (less dependent on church authorities) and less traditional in their conceptions of what it takes to be a good Catholic. The only area where their schooling has fostered a more traditional outlook is abortion.

These results suggest an important paradox. Women and persons with the most Catholic schooling – the most highly committed groups – are most likely to deviate from church teachings. In the struggle between traditional church teachings and secular norms (especially on sexual issues), the Church is losing most among young women and young Catholics with the greatest exposure to Catholic education. Young men and Catholics with less Catholic schooling – who are less involved overall – are most likely to conform to church teachings. This situation leads us to expect tension between church leaders and highly involved Catholic laypeople in the years ahead.

References

D'Antonio, William V. 1994. "The Young and the Restless: A Comparison of Two Generations of Young Catholics" *Conscience*. Autumn: 33-40

Davidson, James D., and Andrea S. Williams. 1993. "Generations of Catholics: Results from Focus Groups." Paper presented at annual meeting of the Association for the Sociology of Religion, Miami.

Fee, Joan L., Andrew M. Greeley, William C. McCready, and Teresa A. Sullivan. 1981. *Young Catholics*. New York: Sadlier.

Greeley, Andrew M. 1989. *Religious Change in America*. Cambridge: Harvard University Press.

Kennedy, Eugene. 1990. *Tomorrow's Catholics, Yesterday's Church*. New York: Harper & Row.

Markey, John J. 1994. "The Making of a Post-Vatican II Theologian: Reflections on 25 Years of Catholic Education." *America*, 16 July: 16-22.

McNamara, Patrick. 1993. *Conscience First, Tradition Second*. Albany: SUNY Press.

Roof, Wade Clark. 1993. *A Generation of Seekers*. San Francisco: Harper.

Williams, Andrea S., and James D. Davidson. 1994. "Diversity in Conceptions of Faith Among Catholics: A Problem of Generations?" Unpublished paper.

6

Women's "Place" in the Church

THE WOMEN'S MOVEMENT, BEGINNING IN THE UNITED STATES IN THE late 1960s, was a catalyst for change in attitude and behavior among all American women. During this same time, Catholic women were also experiencing the changes brought about by the Vatican Council. Hence, it should be no surprise that American Catholic women have changed how they think and feel about their "place" in the Church.

This chapter looks at gender differences in the data from our 1993 study of the Catholic laity and from earlier studies. First we compare women and men regarding commitment to the Church, and then their positions on the teachings of the Church regarding the ordination of women, birth control, abortion, and marriage and divorce. Finally, we examine gender differences in attitudes toward possible parish changes in wake of the priest shortage.

Gender Differences

All Catholic women, including professed women religious, have been excluded from the clerical state, based solely on the fact that they are not males (John Paul II, 1983: Canon 1024). On the other hand, not all Catholic men aspiring to the priesthood can expect to be ordained. One characteristic that might exclude males from the priesthood is in the ability to complete the course of studies required for ordination. Other impediments include marriage, entanglement in public affairs (for example, public office), recent conversion, forms of insanity or psychic defect, heretical beliefs, having murdered, procurement of an abortion, and attempted suicide (John Paul II, 1983: Canons 1041, 1042).

Women's subordinate position as laypersons in the Church is shared by the men in our study, but there is one important difference: men were not born with the doors to the clerical state closed to them, as are women. This means that men have the opportunity, through ordination, to participate in ruling; women do not.[1] We can expect, then, to see some differences in the attitudes and behavior of male and female laity, particularly on issues that impact women.

Commitment

American Catholic women and men respond differently on three subjects closely related to their religion: never leaving the Church, the importance of the Church in their lives, and Mass attendance (see Table 6.1). Given the traditional notion that the mother has the lion's share of responsibility for transmitting religious values to the children, we expect higher percentages among women on all three.

In 1993, 65 percent of the women respondents and 57 percent of the men said they would never leave the Church.[2] Both were *less* likely to say they would never leave the Church than they had said in 1987, men more so than women, but the gender gap has held over the past six years.

Important gender differences occurred, however, with regard to the importance of the Church in one's personal life. A minority of men (37 percent) said that the Church is the "most important" part or "among the most important" parts of their lives, but a full 10 percentage point decrease took place among women (from 59 percent to 49 percent). The gender gap of 20 percent in 1987 became a 12 percent gap in 1993. Women are still more likely than men to say the Church is important in their lives, but the percentages for both have dropped dramatically over the past six years.

The percentages of men and women who say they attend Mass daily or at least weekly is virtually unchanged, a slight decrease of 3 percent. Women (43 percent) are still more likely than men (32 percent) to say they attend Mass weekly or more often, and the gap of 11 percentage points holds.

In summary, then, the data indicate a slight erosion of loyalty and commitment to the Church. Lay women continue to have greater

---

1. Gene Burns, *The Frontiers of Catholicism: The Politics of Ideology in a Liberal World* (Berkeley: University of California Press, 1992): 133. documents the fact that as early as the 1950s some American sisters who were leaders of the Sister Formation Conference questioned the passive images of women that led to their exclusion from important opportunities. This thinking "was a decade ahead of most sisters and of American society as a whole."

2. We asked our respondents to imagine a scale from 1 to 7. At point 1 is the statement, "I would never leave the Catholic Church." At point 7 is the statement, "Yes, I might leave the Catholic Church." Where would you place yourself on that scale? In Table 6.1 we include only those who placed themselves at points 1 and 2 on the scale.

Table 6.1
Catholics' Gender Differences:
Loyalty and Commitment to the Church, 1987 and 1993

Survey Statement Agreed with	Men 1987 (%)	Men 1993 (%)	Women 1987 (%)	Women 1993 (%)
Would never leave Catholic Church	62	57	68	65
Church is most important or among most important parts of your life	39	37	59	49
Attend Mass daily or at least weekly	35	32	46	43

loyalty and commitment to the Church than their male counterparts, but 10 percent fewer said that the Church is an important part of their lives.

Women's Ordination

Three items in our survey tapped attitudes toward women's ordination: whether the laity should participate in deciding whether women should be ordained; whether the policy of ordaining men but not women strengthened their commitment to the Church; and whether it would be a good thing if women were allowed to be ordained as priests (see Table 6.2). We expected that women would show stronger support of women's ordination on all three items because of their own experiences of gender inequality in the Church.

In 1987 men (50 percent) were slightly more likely than women (46 percent) to say that the laity should participate in deciding whether women should be ordained to the priesthood, but in 1993 slightly more women (65 percent) than men (60 percent) responded in this way. What is remarkable on this item is the acceleration of women's positive response, (a 19 percentage point increase) compared to a 10 percentage point increase by the men.

The second item addressed whether the policy of ordaining men but not women strengthened, weakened, or had no effect on the respondent's commitment to the Church. The majority of men and women said that it had no effect; lesser numbers of both said that it *strengthened* their commitment. The latter response denotes those who are *not* in favor of women's ordination, and we can expect that women would be less likely to choose this response. In 1987 women (23 percent) were more likely than men (17 percent) to say that the Church's policy had strengthened their commitment. By 1993 a substantial change had taken place: the men's response remained stable at 16 percent, but significantly fewer women said the Church's policy of ordaining men but not women strengthened their commitment. Between 1987 and 1993, then, gender differences all but disappeared.

Table 6.2
Catholics' Gender Differences:
Women's Ordination, 1985, 1987, and 1993

Survey Statement Agreed with	Men		Women	
	1987 (%)	1993 (%)	1987 (%)	1993 (%)
The laity *should* participate in deciding whether women should be ordained to the priesthood	50	60	46	65
Policy of ordaining men, but not women, to the priesthood *strengthened* your commitment to the Catholic Church	17	16	23	13
	Men		**Women**	
	1985* (%)	1993 (%)	1985* (%)	1993 (%)
Strongly agree or agree somewhat that it would be a good thing if women were allowed to be ordained as priests.	51	67	44	61

*From Dean R. Hoge, *The Future of Catholic Leadership: Responses to the Priest Shortage* (Kansas City, MO: Sheed & Ward, 1987).

The third item attempted to ascertain whether the laity agreed or disagreed with the statement "It would be a good thing if women were allowed to be ordained as priests." Because the question had not been asked in our 1987 survey, we used data from a 1985 survey (Hoge, 1987).

Contrary to our expectations, men were more likely than women to agree in both 1985 and 1993, but the gender differences are not large enough to be considered significant (see Table 6.2). In 1985 the majority (51 percent) of men, and a near majority (44 percent) of women agreed; by 1993 two-thirds of men and almost three-fifths of women agreed. What is important is the increased support for women's ordination over the past eight years among both men (16 percentage points) and women (17 percentage points).

Table 6.3
Catholics' Gender Differences:
Birth Control and Abortion, 1987 and 1993

Survey Statement Agreed with	Men 1987 (%)	Men 1993 (%)	Women 1987 (%)	Women 1993 (%)
The laity *should* have the right to participate in making church policy about birth control.	51	58	54	66
Yes, a person can be a good Catholic without obeying the Church's teaching regarding birth control.	66	71	66	75
Yes, a person can be a good Catholic without obeying the Church's teaching regarding abortion.	45	55	34	56

Birth Control and Abortion

Three questions in our survey addressed the issues of birth control in general and of abortion in particular: the right of the laity to participate in making policy about birth control, and whether a person could be a good Catholic without obeying the Church's teachings regarding birth control and abortion. Assuming that women's lives are more directly involved in these issues because of their child-bearing and child-rearing responsibilities, we expected that laywomen would diverge more from the church's position on birth control and abortion than would laymen.

Larger percentages of women than men said the laity should have the right to participate in Church policy making on birth control, but the gender differences were small. Two-thirds of women and almost three-fifths of men said that laity should have the right. What is important here is the significant increase in the percentage of women supporting the position.

In 1993 three-fourths of women and 71 percent of men said a person can be a good Catholic without obeying the Church's teachings regarding birth control. The gender differences on the issues are almost imperceptible, but again there was greater increase among women over the six-year span than among the men.

We found less questioning of the Church's position on abortion among the laity. In 1987 men (45 percent) were more likely to say one could be a good Catholic without obeying the Church's teaching on abortion than were women (34 percent). By 1993 a majority of both women (56 percent) and men (55 percent) agreed, and the gender difference had virtually disappeared. The percentage point increase over time for the women was 22 percent while for the men it was only 10 percent.

In general, the findings concerning birth control and abortion are that a large majority of men and women question the Church's teachings and want to participate in policy-making on birth control. Women diverge from the Church's teachings only slightly more than men, but the change was much more dramatic in their attitudes over six years than it was among men.

Marriage and Divorce

Our survey included three questions on marriage and divorce: whether a person can be a good Catholic without getting married in the Church; whether a person can be a good Catholic without obeying the Church's teachings regarding divorce and remarriage; and whether the laity should have the right to participate in making Church policy about divorce. In 1993 approximately two-thirds of both women and men diverged from Church teaching on marriage and divorce, and the same proportion supported the laity's right to participate in policy-making (see Table 6.4 and Figure 6.1).

A pattern that we have been noting throughout this chapter emerges again in the first two questions. Men (54 percent) were slightly more likely than women (49 percent) in 1987 to say that a person can be a good Catholic without getting married in the Church, but women were "in the lead" six years later, though the gender differences at both

Table 6.4
Catholics' Gender Differences:
Marriage and Divorce, 1987 and 1993

Survey Statement Agreed with	Men 1987 (%)	Men 1993 (%)	Women 1987 (%)	Women 1993 (%)
Yes, a person can be a good Catholic without getting married in the Church.	54	59	49	64
Yes, a person can be a good Catholic without obeying the Church's teaching regarding divorce and remarriage.	59	58	56	66
Catholic laity *should* have the right to participate in making church policy about divorce.	48	53	52	67

points in time are too small to be considered important. There was a large fifteen point increase in the number of women saying yes on this item in 1993.

Men (59 percent) were slightly more likely than women (56 percent) in 1987 to agree that a person can be a good Catholic without obeying Church teaching regarding divorce and remarriage, but over the next six years there was a gender shift. Women (66 percent) in 1993 were now more likely than men (58 percent) to agree.

In the 1987 survey, there was no notable gender difference on the percentages believing that the laity should have the right to participate in making Church policy about divorce. However, the gender difference of 14 points in 1993 was dramatic, brought on by the increase of 15 points in the women's percentage. Why were women (67 percent) more likely than men (53 percent) to want the laity to participate in policy-making regarding divorce? Possibly Catholic women believe they should be heard on an issue that affects women as well as men because up to the present such is not the case.

Parish Changes and the Priest Shortage

Gender differences in attitudes concerning the priest shortage might be anticipated for two reasons. One, as we pointed out above, women are stronger in loyalty and commitment to the Church, and they

Figure 6.1
Gender Differences, 1987 and 1993, on Four Topics

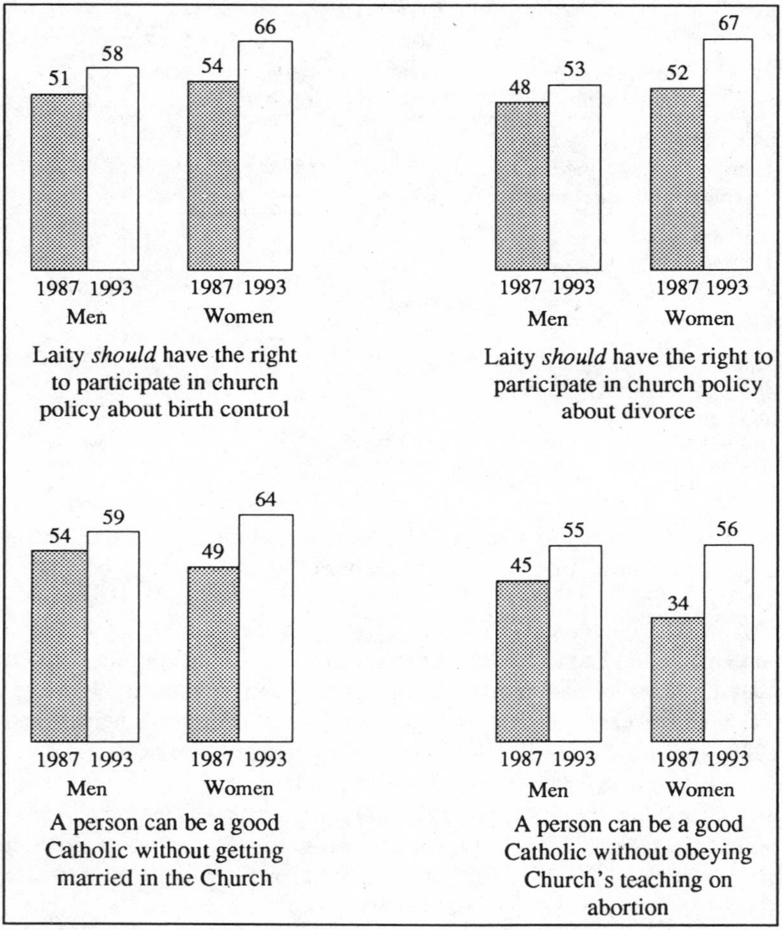

continue to outnumber men in attendance at Mass. Hence we might expect that changes in the local parish would affect them in deeper ways. Two, studies (Murnion, 1992; Wallace, 1992) have shown that more and more women are becoming involved in parish ministry due to the priest shortage, from which might spring greater acceptance of possible parish changes among women.

Items regarding possible changes in the parish due to the priest shortage appeared in the 1985 survey reported on in Hoge (1987) and our 1993 survey (see table 6.5). Keep in mind that the revised code of Canon Law (John Paul II, 1983) had only recently been promulgated at the time of the earlier survey, so the process of including the laity in parish activities was only in its initial stages throughout the country. By 1993 parishioners were beginning to contribute more time to committees in parishes where the priest shortage was acute.

The change least unacceptable in both surveys is having no resident priest in the parish, only a lay parish administrator and visiting priests. Though parishioners accustomed to having a resident priest may resist the idea of having *only* a lay administrator, at least in such a situation they would know that a priest would be available to them. The majority of both men (58 percent) and women (60 percent) resisted this change in 1985, but eight years later fewer men (45 percent) and women (39 percent) said it would be unacceptable. The gender differences are not large enough to be important, but as we have seen, the decrease in women's resistance (21 points) to this change is more notable than men's (13 points).

Table 6.5
Catholics' Gender Differences:
Parish Changes and the Priest Shortage, 1987 and 1993

Prefatory survey statement: If a shortage of priests in the future required a reduction of priestly activities, some changes may occur in parish life. Tell if these changes in your home parish would be very acceptable, somewhat acceptable, or not at all acceptable to you.

Change Not at All Acceptable	Men 1987 (%)	Men 1993 (%)	Women 1987 (%)	Women 1993 (%)
No resident priest in the parish, but only a lay parish administrator and visiting priests.	58	45	60	39
Marriages performed only be deacons or lay officials of the Church.	56	49	63	46
No priest available for visiting the sick.	72	61	76	54
No priest available for administering the Last Rites for the dying.	81	70	85	69

What about having marriages in their parishes performed only by deacons or lay officials of the Church? Although the majority of men (56 percent) and women (63 percent) resisted this change in 1985, eight years later a near majority of men and a sizable minority of women continued to say it was not at all acceptable. Again there were no important gender differences at either time, but there was an important (17 point) decrease in women's resistance.

In 1985 a large majority of both men (72 percent) and women (76 percent) said it was not acceptable to have no priest available for visiting the sick in their parishes, and a majority of both men (61 percent) and women (54 percent) continued to resist this change eight years later. A notable decrease in women's resistance (22 points) appeared once again.

As expected, in 1985 both men (81 percent) and women (85 percent) showed strongest resistance to the situation of no priest available for administering the Last Rites for the dying, and likewise there was virtually no gender difference on this item eight years later, when a large majority of men (70 percent) and women (69 percent) continued to find it not at all acceptable. These data suggest that Catholics persevere in holding as a fundamental right the availability of a priest for the Last Rites in their home parishes.

We introduced a new item in our 1993 survey on a topic that has been emerging with the increase in priestless parishes: communion service led by a layperson as a substitute for Sunday Mass. We asked, "If, due to a shortage of priests, Sunday Mass could not be celebrated, would a Communion service led by a layperson using consecrated hosts be a satisfactory substitute for you?" Thirty percent of men and 27 percent of women replied "Not at all" – much less resistance than to any other of the changes enumerated. This finding may be encouraging to bishops who are beginning to appoint laypersons as parish administrators rather than closing parishes when the supply of priests begins to dwindle.

The revised Code of Canon Law of in 1983 authorizes a bishop to appoint deacons or other persons to administer parishes without resident priests (Canon 517.2). Thus deacons, as well as religious sisters and brothers, and female and male laypersons, have been appointed as pastoral administrators in many countries because of the growing shortage of priests. Among such appointees, deacons are allowed to exercise a wider range of sacramental and liturgical duties, which can be the cause of some tension for women who have been appointed to administer parishes. For instance, when notified that her husband was to be ordained a deacon, a woman who had been sharing the duties of parish administrator with him for four years said: "I am happy for him [her husband], but I am sad for me. I don't think it's fair. It's really hard, that we have been doing this equally together for so long, and now he is to be ordained and I am not" (Wallace, 1992:158).

Looking Back to the Early Church

Although women's "place" in the Church is a heated topic among Catholics today, many people may be unaware that women in the early Church properly engaged in many activities that would be considered the prerogative of members of the clergy today. The role of deaconess is a case in point. A biblical reference to deaconesses in the early Church can be found in Romans 16:1–2, where Paul writes:

> "I commend to you our sister Phoebe, a deaconess of the church at Cenchreae. Give her, in union with the Lord, a welcome worthy of saints, and help her with anything she needs; she has looked after a great many people, myself included."

In the early Church from the first to the fourth centuries deaconesses took part in baptisms by anointing the bodies of the women and accompanying them into the water, and they were charged with instructing the baptized women. Like deacons, they were ordained by the bishop.

Olson (1992:42) explains that women moved more easily into the role of deaconess "during the very early years of the Church when the boundaries between church office and the congregation were less well defined." Also, "the formal office of deaconess surfaced . . . as a solution to the problems of modesty in Christian baptism and visitations of women in the home. The desire of the church to bring its women under the control of the establishment may also have been a motivating factor."

When the diaconate became the final stepping-stone to the priesthood, it resulted in the exclusion of women from the minor orders. Deaconesses became absorbed in the monastic movement, and the position of deaconess had disappeared by the twelveth or thirteenth centuries in Europe, and by the eleventh century in the eastern Mediterranean (Olson, 1992:53, 81). By contrast, many Protestant churches revived the position of deaconess after the Reformation.

Given the decreasing numbers of priests in many parts of the United States, and the need for resources for parish leadership, it is not surprising that the question of the exclusion of women from the diaconate has been raised.[3] Today the consent of a married man's wife is required in order for him to become a deacon, so in that sense women are included. Also, wives of deacons are encouraged to attend the formation sessions with their husbands; those women have virtually completed the formal study required of deacons.

One of our authors (Wallace) interviewed a married woman who was, in fact, the director of the deacon's formation program in her diocese. The anomaly, of course, was that she was heading a program for which she was not eligible. Today, a woman can take the same formation courses as potential deacons and even administer a formation program, but that is as close as she can come to the clerical state.

If women heading parishes were ordained deacons, there would be no need for them to request special permission from a bishop to preach, baptize, witness marriages, or preside at wakes and funeral services. These can be extremely stressful situations for pastor and parishioner alike, as exemplified in the following statement by a nun who was administering a parish:

> I would like to get more involved in the sacraments because I do the preparations for baptism, and I'm not able to do anything in the actual baptism. We have a little boy here who is dying of leukemia, and I spent literally my first two years here with the family, hours and hours. And then when it comes to the funeral, well I did the homily, so I did feel I was part of it. But very often I almost feel as though I am on the outskirts, and I mind that (Wallace, 1992:144).

Likewise, a priest who was the sacramental minister for a parish headed by a woman explained to the congregation during a wedding ceremony:

> I think you all need to know that Sister ______________ is the one who has walked with this couple all these months, and in some way it hurts, when the big day comes, and she steps aside (Wallace, 1992:146).

A parishioner who served as the organist and choir director in a parish headed by a woman expressed her feelings about the sacramental limitations:

> I resent it more and more because she does such a beautiful job. She has done all the footwork. She's done everything. I just feel so frustrated for her, because I just know how I would feel if I prepared all the music, did all the planning, practiced with the folks, and somebody else came in and played the

---

3. See Jeannine E. Olson, *One Ministry/Many Roles: Deacons and Deaconesses through the Centuries* (St. Louis, MO: Concordia, 1992) p. 89 nn. 76, 77, for a discussion of the debate over ordination of deaconesses.

organ and directed, and I sat on the side and watched the whole thing happen (Wallace, 1992:146).

At the present time a special committee of the Canon Law Society of America is preparing a proposal on the admission of women to the diaconate that will be presented at the annual meeting of the society in 1995. As we have seen, ordaining deaconesses would not be inconsistent with practices in the early Church.

Conclusion

In this chapter, we have analyzed survey data that address issues emerging from recent thinking among many Catholics that places increased emphasis on the dignity and gifts of women. Because the issues have been examined in surveys over time, we were able to show the differences between women's and men's attitudes and behavior concerning women's place in the Church.

We found that although women continued to be more committed to the Church than men and attended Mass more often, their commitment decreased over the six-year span. The majority of both women and men became open to change regarding women's ordination, birth control, abortion, marriage, and divorce, but increases in the numbers open to change were higher among women. In fact, there was a "gender shift": women were less open to change than men on these issues in 1987 but were more so six years later.

Given the increased presence of women in ministerial roles because of the decline in numbers of clergy in the United States, we also reported our findings regarding accommodations to the priest shortage on the parish level. Only a minority of men and women viewed the following as unacceptable: Communion service as a substitute for Sunday Mass, a lay administrator in the parish, and marriage performed by a deacon or lay official. On the other hand, the majority of both men and women saw the situations of having no priest available for visiting the sick or for administering the Last Rites as unacceptable. With the exception of the Last Rites situation, however, women were slightly less likely than men to view the accommodations to the priest shortage as unacceptable.

The Vatican Council reforms made it possible for all laypersons to take on new parish roles such as lector and Eucharistic minister;[4]

---

4. For a discussion of changes in the Church since Vatican II, see Helen Rose Ebaugh, ed., *Vatican II and American Catholicism* (Greenwich, CT: Jai Press), 1991.

but the hierarchy has been slow to implement the reforms. This is nowhere better illustrated than in the American bishops' unsuccessful struggle to approve a pastoral letter on the role of women in the Church.

For some Catholic women, the long process of drafting and redrafting of the American bishops' pastoral letter on women contributed to a rethinking about their place in the Church. The final draft entitled "One in Christ Jesus," was rejected as a pastoral letter at the bishops' meeting on 16-19 November 1992, a few months before our survey. The text, which many viewed as a watered-down version of the original, was released as a committee report (U.S. Bishops, 1992), included a denunciation of violence against women and proposals, for example, that all preaching, catechizing, and practice promote the equality and dignity of women, and that each diocese consider establishing a commission on women in the Church and society. However, there was no proposal included for women's ordination to either the diaconate or the priesthood. Still, the fraction of women students in Catholic theological schools has risen steadily from one-fourth in 1988 to one-third in 1993.[5]

By the time of our 1993 survey, greater numbers of women had been elected to Congress, and the new administration's policy of placing women in such top positions as attorney general received considerable media coverage. Subsequent to our survey, the Vatican decision that women can now minister as acolytes was made known, thereby enhancing the likelihood of a female presence at the altar during Mass and other liturgical services. However, Pope John Paul II followed that decision with a declaration prohibiting further discussion of women's ordination. That his directive is likely to engender even more discussion is suggested by the reaction of a grandmother and life-long Catholic to his declaration: "It had more to do with power than with love. I'm embarrassed to be associated with a Church that is so sexist. The Pope's statement is a giant step backward in the movement for equality."[6]

What does the future hold for Catholic women? Will deaconesses reappear in the Church? Will women continue to be denied full participation in all roles and functions within the Church? Will women's increasing awareness that they are second-class citizens in a male-dominated Church, combined with a conviction that change will not occur

---

5. For 1988 data, see William L. Baumgaertner, ed., *Fact Book on Theological Education; 1987-88* (Vandalia, OH: Association of Theological Schools in the United States and Canada, 1988), pp. 90–92. The 1993 enrollment data are from a personal interview on 9 September 1994 with Nancy Merrill, editor of publications, Association of Theological Schools.
6. Personal interview, 5 June 1994.

in their lifetimes, lead to an increasing exodus of women and the loss of their talents to the Church?

We do not know the future, but we are convinced that changes regarding the place of women in the Catholic Church are inevitable. We predict that the following will continue to operate as pressures for change: growing numbers of trained female ministers; insistence on the use of inclusive language; demand for more active leadership roles for women; and in light of the continuing priest shortage, the need to empower and train women for ministry at every level.

References

Baumgaertner, William L., ed. 1988. *Fact Book on Theological Education: 1987–1988*. Vandalia, OH: Association of Theological Schools in the United States and Canada.

Burns, Gene. 1992. *The Frontiers of Catholicism: The Politics of Ideology in a Liberal World*. Berkeley: University of California Press.

Ebaugh, Helen Rose, ed. 1991. *Vatican II and U.S. Catholicism*. Greenwich, CT: JAI Press.

Hoge, Dean R. 1987. *The Future of Catholic Leadership: Responses to the Priest Shortage*. Kansas City, MO: Sheed & Ward.

The Jerusalem Bible. 1966. Garden City, NY: Doubleday.

John Paul II. 1983. *Code of Canon Law*. Washington, D.C.: Canon Law Society of America.

Murnion, Philip J. 1992. *New Parish Ministers: Laity and Religious on Parish Staffs*. New York: National Pastoral Life Center.

Olson, Jeannine E. 1992. *One Ministry/Many Roles: Deacons and Deaconesses through the Centuries*. St. Louis, MO: Concordia.

U.S. Bishops. 1992. "One in Christ Jesus: Ad Hoc Committee Report/Women's Concerns," *Origins* 22, No. 29:489-508.

Wallace, Ruth A. 1992. *They Call Her Pastor: A New Role for Catholic Women*. Albany, NY: SUNY Press.

7

Changes in Parish Life

> We were at a point, as a parish, having established our parish council, where over the years we had come to see that we had to be the church here, because we would either have priests with bad health or no priests. So if the people didn't see to the life of the church, it wasn't going to happen. So we have developed a strong sense of involvement and ownership [Member of a parish council].

This chapter discusses changes that have taken place in parishes throughout the United States since 1965, when Vatican Council II adjourned. We begin with three key factors that have encouraged the pressure for parish restructuring: the influence of the Council decrees, changes in church law, and the priest shortage. Using data from our 1993 survey as well as other earlier studies, we then turn to a report on the attitudes of the Catholic laity on two topics: new forms of pastoral leadership, and participation in parish life.

Vatican II

Two of the issues addressed by the Second Vatican Council that served to pave the way for parish changes were the emphasis on the "signs of the times" and the definition of the Church as the "People of God." In convoking the council, Pope John XXIII used the image of the "signs of the times," a phrase frequently used by him, and taken from Matthew 16:4 where Jesus is asked by the Pharisees and Sadducees if he would show them a sign from heaven. Jesus said: "In the evening you say, 'It will be fine; there is a red sky,' and in the morning, 'Stormy weather today; the sky is red and overcast.' You know how to read the face of the sky, but you cannot read the signs of the times." In summoning the council, John XXIII stated on 25 December 1961 (Abbott, 1966:704): "Indeed, we make ours the recommendation of Jesus that one should know how to distinguish the 'signs of the times,' and we seem to see now, in the midst of so much darkness, a few indications which augur well for the fate of the Church and of humanity."

Clearly, the delegates at Vatican II "got the message," for the introductory statement of the council document entitled "The Pastoral Constitution on the Church in the Modern World" includes the following (Abbott, 1966:201-202):

> To carry out such a task, the Church has always had the duty of scrutinizing the signs of the times and of interpreting them in the light of the gospel. Thus, in language intelligible to each generation, she can respond to the perennial questions which men ask about this present life and the life to come, and about the relationship of the one to the other. We must therefore recognize and understand the world in which we live, its expectations, its longings and its often dramatic characteristics.

Reference is made later to profoundly changed conditions in the world and the importance of social science research projects (like ours) to an understanding of the "signs of the times" (Abbott, 1966:203): "Advances in biology, psychology, and the social sciences not only bring men hope of improved self-knowledge. In conjunction with technical methods, they are also helping men to exert direct influence on the life of social groups."[1]

Another outcome of Vatican II that signaled an openness to change was the new definition of the Church as "the People of God." In fact, the second of the council documents "Dogmatic Constitution on the Church" is entitled "The People of God." By using this term, the council put greater emphasis on the communal side of the Church rather than its hierarchical or institutional aspects. The term refers to the total community of the church, including all female and male laypersons as well as clergy (Abbott, 1966:24,25). The implications for the role of the laity in the life of the parish are evidenced in the following statement by a parishioner: "I feel part of the Church now. I didn't feel part of the Church before. The priest did everything; he did all the thinking. Now the responsibility has been sent down to us and in our parish it is working great. I am encouraged. I love it. It's our Church" (Wallace, 1992:89).

---

1. The use of the image of the "signs of the times" by Pope John XXIII, as Burns (1992:56) points out, is closely related to the principle of the development of doctrine. To strengthen his argument that the development of doctrine has been institutionalized within Catholic ideology, Burns cites its use by Pope Paul VI in *Populorum Progressio* (1967) and by the American bishops in justifying their increased attention to the morality of nuclear policy in the 1980s.

The council's attention to the "signs of the times," and the expansion of the concept of the Church to embrace the laity as well as clergy aided the efforts in some parts of the world to empower the laity on the parish level. An example of this inclusion comes from an interview with a parish leader in a rural area in the United States (Wallace, 1992:88):

> We had a group of parishioners that studied some of the documents on Vatican II that said the people are the Church. That was a whole new experience to think of yourselves as Church because we always knew that the priests and nuns were the Church and the rest of you were just there. So we went through a number of months of formation, forming the parish council, and beginning to say, 'We are the Church.'

Changes in Church Law

Church law refers to the rules by which the practical life of the Church is governed, and it is designated by the term "canon," from the Greek word for rule. Although John XXIII convened the first session of the Second Vatican Council in 1962, he had been well aware of the importance of changes in church law for implementation of the council decrees. In anticipation of this need, he called for the revision of canon law in 1959, and soon committees made up of bishops and canon lawyers were formed for this purpose. Committees spent many years analyzing the decrees of Vatican II, and then making changes that would bring the new Code of Canon Law in line with the Vatican II documents. The new Code of Canon Law was promulgated in 1983.

One example of the legal changes that encouraged change on the parish level is found in Canon 208: "In virtue of their rebirth in Christ there exists among all the Christian faithful a true equality with regard to the dignity and activity whereby all cooperate in the building up of the Body of Christ in accord with each one's own condition and function."[2] It carries a suggestion of an empowerment of the laity, but the laity's share of authority remains far from equal to that of the pastor in most parishes.

Another legal change that was particularly important in opening the door for parish restructuring can be found in Canon 517.2, which reads:

> If the diocesan bishop should decide that due to a dearth of priests a participation in the exercise of the pastoral care of a parish is to be entrusted to a deacon or to some other person

2. *Code of Canon Law* (Washington, D.C.: Canon Law Society of America, 1983).

> who is not a priest, or to a community of persons, he is to appoint some priest endowed with the power and faculties of a pastor, to supervise the pastoral care.[3]

Clearly, the driving force for this parish change was the priest shortage, which we discuss in the next section. Some of the bishops and canon lawyers on the committee that proposed the change embodied in Canon 517.2 "did not welcome the notion that a parish be entrusted, even in part" to a nonordained person. It was Venezuelan Archbishop Rosalio Jose Castillo Lara who convinced the committee not to exclude nonordained persons in the wording of the new canon by vividly describing the effectiveness of the pastoral care in parishes entrusted to religious sisters in his diocese, where the priest shortage was particularly acute. The proposed canon was approved (Renken, 1987).

The Priest Shortage

The best source for a thorough understanding of the extent of the shortage of priests in the United States is found in a nationwide study by sociologists Richard A. Schoenherr and Lawrence A. Young (1993), *Full Pews and Empty Altars: Demographics of the Priest Shortage in United States Catholic Dioceses*. In 1966, 35,070 diocesan priests were active; Schoenherr and Young (p. 57) predict that by the year 2005 there will be approximately 21,030, a 40 percent loss. They also predict a 65 percent increase in demand for priestly services because of a continuing increase in church membership: between 1965 and 1985, for example, membership reportedly grew from 44,790,000 to 64,341,000. Because of high fertility rates and the increased immigration of Latino and Asian immigrants, Schoenherr and Young (p. 298) predict that by 2005 the membership will reach 74,109,000. (See Figure 7.1).

How will the projected numbers affect the ratio of priest to parishioner? In 1975 the ratio was 1:1,100; Schoenherr and Young (1993:3) conservatively see its doubling by 2005: "The diminishing size of the priest population is the major driving force for social change within late 20th-century Catholicism."

The title of the Schoenherr and Young volume, *Full Pews and Empty Altars*, is, of course, hyperbole. Our studies and those of others make clear that the pews are nowhere near as full as they were some thirty years ago. Whether a majority of the new Catholics will be found

---

3. Ibid.

Figure 7.1
Numbers of Diocesan Priests and Catholic Church Members in the United States: 1966-2005.

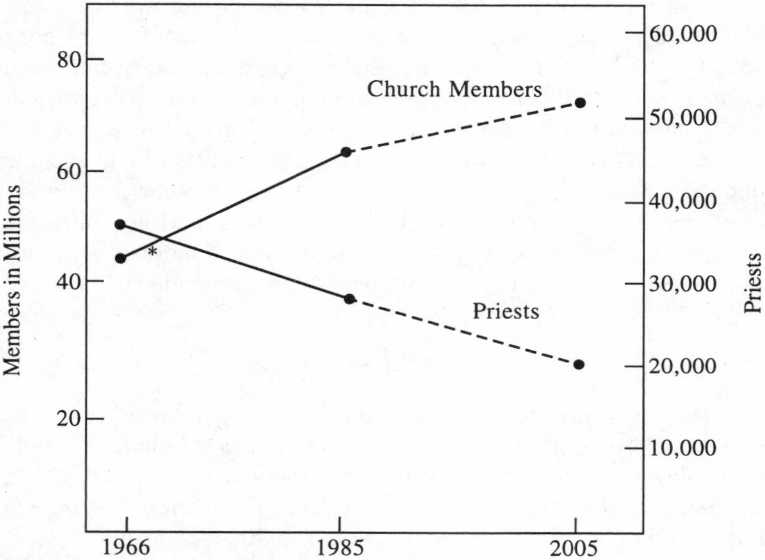

Sources: For priests, Schoenherr and Young (1993: 57). For members, Gallup polls, cited in Schoenherr and Young (1993:298).

*1965 data.

in the pews by 2005 is doubtful, given attendance trends.[4] But the title does point to the growing crisis concerning the central position on the altar in the Catholic Church in the United States, if the position is reserved for only a celibate male priest. Some solutions to the "empty altars" problem that are in either the planning stages or already in effect include the closing of parishes, leaving parishes vacant, building larger churches in order to accommodate more parishioners with fewer Masses, bringing in priests from other countries as pastors, and saying special prayers for vocations to the priesthood.

Other solutions nearer at hand are more realistic and less devastating for parishioners who desperately want to keep their parishes

---

4. With regard to the problem of "full pews," our data show that regular Mass attendance has dropped from 75% in the 1950s to 41% in 1993, and even lower among younger laity between 18 and 34 years old, only 24% of whom said that they attended Mass at least weekly. See Chapter 4.

open: married male priests, female priests, and lay pastoral administrators.

Lay Attitudes Toward Potential New Forms of Pastoral Leadership

Married Priests

In our 1993 survey we asked laypersons to tell us whether they agreed with this statement: "It would be a good thing if married men were allowed to be ordained as priests." Overall, 72 percent agreed strongly or somewhat, 9 percentage points more than in 1985, and 20 percentage points more than in 1970 (see Figure 7.2). Groups with percentages over 80 percent in our 1993 survey included upper class ($50,000 or more yearly income), less-than-once-a-week Mass attenders, midwesterners, and college graduates.

Recent data from a *Los Angeles Times* (1994:11) national survey of Catholic priests and nuns show that the majority are also in favor of allowing priests to marry, though slightly less than the laity. Priests showed a 59 percent approval rate; nuns, 66 percent.

Women Priests

We also sought the opinions of our lay respondents of another possible resource, women priests, using a similar statement: "It would be a good thing if women were allowed to be ordained as priests." Overall, 64 percent agreed, a dramatic increase from 1974, when only 29 percent had agreed (see Figure 7.2). Fifty-three percent of our sample's most committed Catholics also agreed. (See Chapter 8 for more details on the most committed Catholics.)

Another statement in our survey probed opinion on women's ordination: "Since the original leaders of the Church were men, women should not be ordained to the priesthood." Thirty-one percent agreed, but the majority (67 percent) disagreed. Overall, then, about two-thirds of the Catholic laity, including 62 percent of the most committed Catholics, would accept women priests in their parishes. Our survey did not include religious sisters or priests, but we have some evidence of their stand on this issue from the *Los Angeles Times* (1994) poll, which found a majority of nuns (57 percent) approving of women priests, but less than a majority of priests (44 percent) approving.

Figure 7.2
Percent of Catholics Agreeing
that Women and Married Men Should Be Ordained

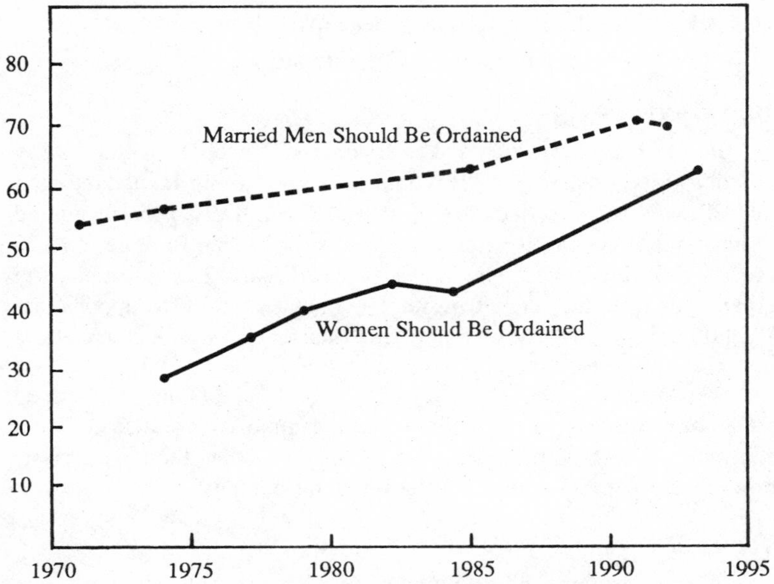

Sources: For women, Gallup polls compiled by the Quixote Center, Hyattsville, Maryland; Gallup polls in 1993. For married men, Gallup poll CO7187 from the Roper Center; Hoge (1987); CSO/Gallup poll in 1992.

Lay Parish Leaders

As we explained above, both the priest shortage and the new law allowing bishops to entrust parishes to deacons and laypersons encouraged bishops to search for solutions to vacant parishes. Since 1983, when the new Code of Canon Law was promulgated, bishops worldwide have begun to appoint non-priests (deacons, nuns, brothers, and laypersons) to head parishes. By 1992 close to 40 percent of the dioceses in the United States had at least one parish headed by a non-priest, and seventeen dioceses have five or more such parishes. In 1994 the total number of parishes headed by persons other than priests was 308, which is 2 percent of all U.S. parishes. Fifty-six percent of these new parish leaders are nuns; 15 percent deacons; 8 percent brothers; 10 percent laywomen; 4 percent laymen; and 8 percent pastoral teams, which usually serve a number of parishes, and typically include laypersons, deacon, and priest. Adding the religious sisters to laywomen, we can see that these new parish leaders are predominantly (66 percent) female.

A priest who served as a sacramental minister in a parish headed by a woman reflected on her ministry:

> What I sense is that she is able to plug in, to express, or open up, or invite a different part of people than what probably most priests would touch. She is able to feel more what especially the women of the parish – what's happening to them and within them and their lives, and the experiences they are having. I think she is able to identify better with that. And also with men, in some ways. (Wallace, 1992:61)

Because entrusting parishes to non-priests is a growing phenomenon, we were interested in respondents' reactions to their own parishes' possible loss of a resident priest. We presented the following statement in 1993:

> If a shortage of priests in the future required a reduction of priestly activities, some changes may occur in parish life. I am going to read a list of six changes which may occur. Please tell me after each if you would be willing to accept it in your home parish. Tell me if it would be very acceptable, somewhat acceptable, or not at all acceptable to you.

Table 7.1 combines the "very acceptable" and "somewhat acceptable" responses. Because this question was asked on an earlier survey in 1985 (Hoge, 1987), we were able to look at trends.

Assuming that most Catholics who are accustomed to having a priest resident pastor in the parish would not welcome changes pursuant to his absence, we did not expect to have a majority of the respondents accepting them. Nonetheless, three changes were either very or somewhat acceptable to our respondents (see Table 7.1). The most acceptable accommodation was "baptisms performed only by deacons or lay officials of the Church"; 63 percent of the laity accepted this change, an increase of 7 percentage points since the 1985 survey. Given that the Church allows baptism by laypersons in emergencies, this outcome is not surprising. The second item with a majority acceptance (56 percent) was "no resident priest in the parish, but only a lay administrator and visiting priests"; in 1985, only 39 percent had signified its acceptability. Finally, 51 percent of our respondents said they would accept "marriages performed only by deacons or lay officials of the Church," an increase of 13 percentage points.

Note that the first and third items in table 7.1 include the word deacon; the second does not. This new form of parish leadership represents another change initiated by the Vatican Council. It was not until Vatican II convened in the mid-1960s that the issue of the diaconate as a permanent ministry, rather than a transitional phase before priestly ordination, was raised to the level of official debate. A majority of the council delegates voted to restore the diaconate as a permanent ministry, and the restoration was approved by Pope Paul VI on 18 June 1967.[5]

In the apostolic letter "The Sacred Order of Deacons: General Norms for Restoring the Permanent Diaconate in the Latin Church" (August 1972), Pope Paul VI outlined two types of permanent deacons: 1) men 25 years or older who remain celibate, have three years of formal study, and serve full-time; and 2) men 35 years or older who, if married, have the consent of their wives to become deacons (but they cannot remarry if widowed), who have studied for an unspecified amount of time and who work as deacons part-time along with practicing their own professions.

On 1 January 1973, Pope Paul VI's letter "First Tonsure, Minor Orders and the Subdiaconate" took effect. Changes included the following: elimination of the subdiaconate, thereby joining the diaconate to the clerical state; changing the minor orders of lector and acolyte to ministries, and opening the ministries of lector and acolyte to laymen. By 1992 more than 17,000 deacons were serving in 105 countries, 10,000 in the United States.

The sacramental and liturgical activities of deacons in Catholic churches include baptizing, witnessing marriages, presiding at wakes, leading word-and-Communion services, and blessing persons, houses, and objects of private devotion. Deacons wear an alb and stole during Mass, and assist the priest by leading the congregation in the opening penitential rite; reading the Gospel; preaching; leading the prayers of intercession; holding the chalice while the priest holds the host after the consecration; inviting the congregation to exchange the greeting of peace, participating in the distribution of the Eucharist; and dismissing the congregation. The only activities in which deacons may not engage is the celebration of the Mass, the anointing of the sick, and the pronouncing of absolution.

Social ministries of deacons include visiting the sick and imprisoned, teaching, counseling, leading retreats, marriage preparation, assisting in annulment processes, and inner-city works, poverty programs,

---

5. See Olson's (1992) chapter on "Permanent Deacons and Contemporary Trends," pp. 355-366 for an expanded discussion of the permanent diaconate in the Catholic Church. Much of the material in the remaining parts of this section are drawn from it.

and soup kitchens. Laypersons participate in these social ministries as well, but as mentioned above, are excluded from the sacramental and liturgical activities. Hence, it is not surprising that parishioners tend to view the deacon's position in the parish as a "cut above" their own.

Although our survey showed a majority of Catholics accepting lay parish administrators, and baptisms and marriages performed by deacons or lay officials, they were much less open to three other possible accommodations to the priest shortage in their home parishes (Table 7.1). Only 41 percent were willing to accept the following two accommodations to the priest shortage: "reducing the number of Masses to less than once a week," and having "no priest available for visiting the sick." But in both cases, there were significant increases (13 and 17 percentage points, respectively) over 1985.

The change that was least acceptable to our respondents was having "no priest available for administering the last rites for the dying"; only 30 percent said it was acceptable. In 1985, 15 percent had said it was so, which means the percentage of laity open to change has doubled in the eight year span.

In general, we found that the laity's acceptance of all six of the possible changes in their parishes due to the priest shortage has increased since 1985. Although there are variations among regions, American Catholics as a whole are becoming more aware of the decline in the number of priests available for parish leadership and the consequent imperilment of the viability of their parishes. Thus, they see a restructuring of parish leadership as a means to continue as a parish. These data on lay attitudes toward parish changes are among the "signs of the times" that may be helpful to bishops who are or will be making decisions about closing or amalgamating parishes, recruiting priests from another country, or appointing lay administrators to some of the parishes without resident priests.

Another change that is already happening in countries experiencing the priest shortage is substitution of a "word-and-communion service" for a Mass when a priest is unavailable. Clearly, Catholics in general would prefer to attend a Mass, especially on Sunday (or Saturday evening), rather than a Communion service. Research on priestless parishes has shown that parishioners tend to become less resistant, however, after experiencing the reality of a word-and-communion service, during which they pray, hear Scripture followed by a homily, and receive consecrated Hosts preserved from a previous Mass (Gilmour, 1986; Wallace, 1992).

Table 7.1
Acceptable Parish Accommodations to Priest Shortage

Parish Accommodation	1985 (%)	1993 (%)
Baptisms performed by deacons or lay officials	56	63
No resident priest, only lay administrator and visiting priest	39	56
Marriages performed by deacons or lay officials	38	51
Less than one Mass a week	28	41
No priest to visit sick	24	41
No priest for Last Rites	15	30

Note: Figures for 1985 are from Dean R. Hoge, *The Future of Catholic Leadership* (Kansas City, MO: Sheed & Ward, 1987).

A religious sister who headed a parish reflected on the meaning of her ministry, in particular her opportunities to preach during the word-and-communion service:

> I think the people and an inner call are what keep me going in my ministry. I really think the Spirit is the one who speaks through me. I prepare because I really love preparing my Sunday liturgies as best I can. Once I have it all written and all prepared, I say, "Lord, it is your job." And He/She takes over. (Wallace, 1992:170)

We were very interested in lay reactions to word-and-communion services, so the survey question asked, "If, because of a shortage of priests, Sunday Mass could not be celebrated, would a Communion service led by a layperson using consecrated hosts be a satisfactory substitute for you?" The response categories were "on a regular basis, on occasion, or not at all." Fifty-four percent said that it would be a satisfactory substitute *on occasion*; only 16 percent would accept it *on a regular basis*; and 29 percent replied *not at all.*

The regional differences on this subject are instructive because the dioceses where bishops have appointed non-priests to head parishes are in the Midwest, the South, and the West (Wallace, 1992:17). For instance, dioceses with five or more parishes headed by persons other than priests include Indianapolis, Toledo, Saginaw, Gaylord, La Crosse, and New Ulm in the Midwest; Jackson, Jefferson City, Knoxville, Raleigh, and Richmond in the South; and Anchorage, Fairbanks, Seattle, and Spokane in the West. Parishioners in the East have had less experience attending word-and-Communion services on the weekend because of the continued availability of priests. Although none of the regions shows a majority accepting such services as a regular practice, (57 percent) in the Midwest, South, and West would accept it on occasion, compared with 49 percent in the East. An even more striking difference is found on total non-acceptance of the practice: 35 percent of the respondents in the East replied "not at all," compared to 25 percent of those in the other three regions, where there is a greater possibility that Catholics have attended such a service, talked to others who have, or read about it in their diocesan papers. We predict, accordingly, that fewer parishioners will be wholly unaccepting of the word-and-Communion service as a substitute in the next few years, as bishops countrywide entrust more and more parishes to non-priests.

Lay Attitudes Toward Participation in Parish Life

If lay Catholics are viewing the Church as the People of God, and are beginning to say, in increasing numbers, "We are the Church," then we can expect them to want to participate more in parish life. Recent research has already documented increasing lay empowerment in churches throughout the country.

Philip Murnion (1992) surveyed pastors, lay and religious parish ministers employed in the parish at least twenty hours a week, other staff, and parishioners in parishes throughout the United States. The total number of parish ministers interviewed was 974, of whom 85 percent were women (44 percent, laywomen; 41 percent, religious sisters); 14 percent were laymen; and 1 percent religious brothers. The roles and activities included religious education (40 percent); pastoral associates (27 percent); music ministers (8 percent); youth ministers (8 percent); liturgy (5 percent); concerns such as ministry to the sick and elderly, social ministry, spirituality, or evangelization (11 percent); and parish administrators, that is, heads of parishes (1 percent). Compensation for the full-time ministerial positions ranged from $11.77 an hour for liturgists to $8.03 an hour for those in the more encompassing category.

Given the extent of the priest shortage in the United States, it is not surprising that parishioners' skills are being tapped more frequently in an effort to keep parishes open. In addition to the jobs mentioned above, parishioners also continue to serve their parishes in more traditional roles like groundskeeper, secretary, and housekeeper.

Aware that more and more parishioners are participating in the ongoing work of parishes, we were interested in the laypersons' attitudes toward their right to participate in policy-making at the parish level. The following statement probed the issue: "For each of the following areas of church life, please tell me if you think the Catholic laity should have the right to participate, or should not have the right to participate." Two of the policy issues pertained directly to parish life, and it is these two that we discuss.

There continued to be overwhelming support for the right to participate in "how parish income is spent" (83 percent in 1993; 81 percent in 1987). In 1993 support reached 88 percent and 90 percent, respectively, among Catholics with incomes in excess of $40,000 annually and among college graduates.

The other parish policy issue concerned selection of the parish priest. In 1993, 74 percent said that the laity should have the right to participate in the process, compared to 57 percent in 1987 – an increase of roughly one third over the past six years.

Important differences on the support for the right to select parish priests were found on several characteristics: *Importance of the Catholic Church*, that is, those who said it was not important (88 percent) compared with those who said the Church was important (71 percent); *Mass attendance*, that is, those who attend less than once a week (81 percent wanted to select their priests), compared with those who attend at least once a week (66 percent); and *age*, that is, those 18 to 54 (80 percent), compared with those 55+ (58 percent).

Why should Catholics who attend Mass less than once a week and for whom the Church is not important express stronger support for the right to select parish priests than those who are more committed? Ideally, such Catholics should be interviewed personally and in some depth on this matter in order to understand their definition of the situation. At this point we can speculate that even though they may place themselves at the periphery of the Church, they value autonomy within all social organizations, including the Church. Again, it is important to keep in mind that all of the responses were in the majority, and most of them fell in the 70 to 80 percent range.

We were also interested in parishioner commitment. We asked, "In the past five years, has your commitment to your local parish changed? Have you become more committed, less committed, or has there been no change?" Half said that there had been no change in their commitment, and the percentages on the "more committed" (23 percent) and "less committed" (25 percent) responses were almost equally divided. However, there was one important difference among the "less committed": 33 percent of the 18-to-34 year olds said that their commitment had lessened over the past five years, compared to 19 percent of those who were 35 and older. Whether the growing empowerment of the laity at the parish level will increase the commitment of the younger members of the parish is unknown at this point.

Conclusion

Vatican II council deliberations – particularly on the definition of the Church as the People of God, the importance of looking at the signs of the times, and the principle of collegiality – have affected the attitudes of the contemporary Catholic laity. In addition, the growing priest shortage has led to new developments in parish life, resulting in a growing empowerment of the laity, including the administration of parishes without a resident priest.

Pope John Paul II (1994:42) is wary of these developments. In public statements in 1987, 1993, and 1994 he cautioned against increasing the community of the Church by "clericalizing" laypersons and "laicizing" priests. Arguing that just as a shepherd cannot be replaced by one of his flock, a lay administrator's services and ministries are never "properly speaking" pastoral. Exercising tasks heretofore the province of the pastoral ministry "does not make pastors of the lay faithful."

We expect that an increase in active participation will be an ongoing challenge for lay Catholics. Some bishops will continue to encourage lay participation: others will opt for other solutions to the problem of scarce resources by recruiting priests from other countries and/or encouraging prayers for priestly vocations. Echoing the words of Pope John XXIII, we are convinced that the future of parish life depends on how we – the People of God, clergy and laity – "know how to distinguish the 'signs of the times.'"

References

Abbott, Walter M. 1966. *The Documents of Vatican II*. New York: America.

Burns, Gene. 1992. *The Frontiers of Catholicism: The Politics of Ideology in a Liberal World*. Berkeley: University of California.

Gilmour, Peter. 1986. *The Emerging Pastor: Non-ordained Catholic Pastors*. Kansas City, MO: Sheed & Ward.

Hoge, Dean R. 1987. *The Future of Catholic Leadership*. Kansas City, MO: Sheed & Ward.

The Jerusalem Bible. 1966. Garden City, NY: Doubleday.

John Paul II. 1983. *Code of Canon Law*. Washington, D.C.: Canon Law Society of America.

John Paul II. 1994. "Do Laity Share in the Priest's Pastoral Ministry?" *Origins* 24.3:42.

Los Angeles Times. 1994. "Los Angeles Times Survey of Roman Catholic Priests and Nuns in the United States," (February 20-22).

Murnion, Phillip J. 1992. *New Parish Ministers: Laity and the Religious on Parish Staffs*. New York: National Pastoral Life Center.

The Official Catholic Directory. 1992. New York: Kenedy.

Olson, Jeannine E. 1992. *One Ministry/Many Roles: Deacons and Deaconesses through the Centuries*. St. Louis, MO: Concordia.

Renken, John A. 1987. "Canonical Issues in the Pastoral Care of Parishes without Priests." *The Jurist*. 47:506-519.

Schoenherr, Richard A., and Laurence A. Young. 1993. *Full Pews and Empty Altars: Demographics of the Priest Shortage in the United States Catholic Dioceses*. Madison: University of Wisconsin.

Wallace, Ruth A. 1992. *They Call Her Pastor: A New Role for Catholic Women*. Albany, NY: SUNY.

8

The Most-Committed American Catholics

SURVEYS OF THE AMERICAN CATHOLIC POPULATION HAVE CONSISTENTLY shown growing majorities to have views on a variety of issues that distance them from the positions of the Vatican and the U.S. bishops. Some critics have insisted that the surveys distort reality by including in their numbers people who are only marginally Catholic. That is, the surveys include people who still identify themselves as Catholics when asked but who seldom go to Mass, and whose behavior in no major way distinguishes them as Catholic. Accordingly, a survey of highly committed Catholics would show strong support for the teachings of the magisterium. Is there a distinct difference in attitudes and behavior between the Church's most committed members and those who are much less committed?

From our 1987 and 1993 surveys we selected three measures of individual commitment: 1) Mass attendance; 2) importance of the Church in the life of the individual; and 3) the individual's readiness to leave the Church. Our preliminary analysis of these variables suggested that on a range of issues, including democratic decision-making, moral authority, sexuality and related family matters, and ordination of women and married persons, views accord with level of commitment. However, in 1987 the most highly committed did not give automatic support to the official teachings, and by 1993 there was further erosion. This occurred even though the U.S. bishops, with financial aid from the Knights of Columbus, were making a special effort to convince the laity of the evil of abortion. And Pope John Paul II continued his condemnation of birth control, divorce, and abortion, and repeatedly insisted on the rightness of the Church's teachings on all matters, among them a celibate clergy and the limited role of women.

Measures of Commitment

We identified three levels of commitment among the laity: high, moderate, and low; following Fichter (1951; 1954), we call them Nuclear Catholics, Modal Catholics, and Dormant Catholics. The Nuclear Catholics are those in the 1987 and 1993 samples who 1) said they attended Mass at least once a week, 2) said the Church was one of the most important influences on their lives, and 3) on a 7-point scale, checked point 1 or 2 that they would never leave the Church. Twenty-three percent of the sample gave these responses in 1993; 27 percent in 1987. Thus, approximately one in four Catholics in both surveys said he or she was highly committed to the Church.

We then separated out the least committed Catholics (the Dormants). We had expected a fairly high overlap among the criteria; that is, people who said they seldom or never went to Mass would also be expected to say the Church was not important in their lives. And we expected them most often to say that they might leave the Church (points 5 to 7 on the scale). Only 7 percent of the 1993 sample responded in such ways. For our purposes, then, it seemed more appropriate to expand the low commitment category, which we did by including those who gave the lowest commitment response on any two of the three variables. This yielded 16 percent of the 1987 sample and 21 percent of the 1993 sample. In effect, only one in five Catholics falls in the Dormant category in terms of these criteria.

The middle category, Modal Catholics, said they went to Mass at least monthly; said the Church was quite important to them, as were other organizations; and checked points 3 and 4 on the 7-point scale of whether they might leave the Church. In 1987 the category constituted 58 percent of the sample; in 1993, 56 percent.

Independent support for our indicators may be garnered from several studies. Hadaway, Marler, and Chaves (1993) reported that actual counts of Mass attendance suggest that only 28 percent of Catholics are "regulars," in contrast to survey reports of as high as 50 percent (Woodward, 1993:80,82). The 28 percent figure for the Nuclear Catholics is close to our figures (27 percent and 23 percent). Further, Woodward reported that studies using a variety of criteria by which to characterize level of religious commitment concluded that only one in six Catholics could be said to be highly committed. At the other end, they found that almost a third were basically secular. Hence, our three categories seem reasonable.

Who Are They? Nuclear, Modal and Dormant Catholics

Two-thirds of the Nuclear Catholics were forty years or older in 1987 and in 1993. In general, the Nuclears were older than the Modal and Dormant Catholics; much more likely to be women; more likely to be married and less likely to be single; more likely to have had a Catholic high school but not grade school education; about as likely to have had education beyond high school; roughly as evenly distributed across income lines; more evenly distributed across the East, Midwest and South; and less likely to be found in the West.

In both surveys women significantly outnumbered men among the Nuclears; however, the proportion dropped from 69 percent in 1987 to 62 percent in 1993. And the finding that the smallest percentage of highly committed came from the West is consonant with other research suggesting that the West is the least formally religious region of the U.S. (Stark & Bainbridge, 1985: Chapter 4; Kosmin and Lachman, 1993:82-85).

The committed and uncommitted laity were similar in overall education level and in the percentages who attended Catholic grade school, but dissimilar in high school education. More Nuclears had attended Catholic high school, but because less than 40 percent had done so, such schooling can be considered at best only as one possible influence on level of commitment. In 1987 and 1993 the three categories differed little in family income.

The Modal Catholics were almost evenly split in age and sex grouping. They were as likely as the Nuclears to have had at least some college, slightly more than half were married in both surveys, and one in four was single.

The two characteristics most distinctive of the Dormant Catholics were age and sex. They were clearly the youngest of the three categories and had strong male majorities in both surveys. They were the least likely to be married, and slightly more likely to be divorced or separated.

Beliefs and Practices

In both surveys we asked if respondents' commitment to the Church was strengthened, weakened, or unaffected by Church teachings that contraception and abortion are wrong, by the policy of ordaining only men as priests, or by the homosexual tendencies or sexual abuses of some priests. Nuclear Catholics were consistent in both surveys on

Table 8.1
Demographic Profile of Catholic Laity, by Level of Commitment, 1987 and 1993

	1987			1993		
	Nuclear (%)	Modal (%)	Dormant (%)	Nuclear (%)	Modal (%)	Dormant (%)
Age						
18-29	17	33	34	41	28	39
30-39	18	23	34	18	25	31
40-54	21	20	21	27	22	23
55+	44	24	11	42	25	8
Education						
Some high school	21	22	19	22	19	18
High school graduate	41	41	36	36	40	40
Some college	18	20	23	20	22	17
College graduate	11	11	15	13	13	16
Graduate school	8	6	8	9	7	8
Catholic grade school	56	53	45	58	47	57
Catholic high school	31	24	18	37	21	18
Sex						
Male	31	50	65	38	50	56
Female	69	50	35	62	50	44
Marital Status						
Married	74	57	65	64	52	48
Divorced/ Separated	6	9	13	12	13	17
Widowed	6	7	4	12	9	3
Single	14	27	19	12	26	32
Income						
<$20,000	30	31	21	45	40	39
$20-39,000	32	30	39	32	37	39
$40,000+	38	39	40	23	23	23
Region						
East	42	38	48	31	38	42
Midwest	19	17	14	28	20	18
South	19	17	14	31	20	20
West	15	18	19	10	21	19

all responses: they were the most likely to say their commitment was strengthened by the Church's teachings on contraception and abortion, and by the Church's policy of ordaining only men. One in four said commitment was weakened by media accounts of homosexuality and sexual abuse among priests.

Dormants were the most likely to say their commitment was weakened by the Church's teachings on contraception and abortion and its policy of ordaining only men. Their responses in both 1987 and 1993 were fairly consistent.

Modal Catholics split; they were more likely to say their commitment was weakened by the teaching on contraception; were about evenly divided on the policy of ordaining men only; and more likely to say their commitment was strengthened by the Church's teaching on abortion.

Apparently, the Church's efforts to defend its teachings had borne some fruit, especially among Nuclear Catholics. This was clearly the case on abortion; in both surveys a majority of Nuclears said they were strongly encouraged by the Church's teachings. Also, more Modals said their commitment was strengthened rather than weakened by the teachings. At the same time, all categories continued to separate contraception from abortion. In contrast, reports of homosexual tendencies and sexual abuse by some priests had the effect of weakening commitment for all three groups.

Our 1987 and 1993 surveys also sought to ascertain who should have moral authority on issues relating to sexuality and marriage: Church leaders alone; the laity alone, taking Church and other teachings into account; or the laity working with church leaders (see Table 8.2 and Figure 8.1).

The responses of the Nuclears were fairly consistent between 1987 and 1993 on two items: divorce and remarriage without an annulment, and the use of contraceptive birth control. On the former only one in three thought moral authority should belong to church leaders alone; one in five chose the individual layperson; and some 40 percent thought both should work together. On contraception, nearly half saw it as a matter for the individual only, while one in four gave support to its being the province of church leaders alone.

More telling, perhaps, were changes on three other items between 1987 and 1993: abortion, extramarital sex, and homosexual behavior. A significant number of Nuclears moved from looking to the magisterium alone to the position that these were matters for shared decision-making by church leaders and the laity. By 1993 on none of the

Table 8.2
Catholic Lay Opinion on Locus of Moral Authority on Sexual and Marital Issues by Commitment, 1987 and 1993

	Nuclear (%)			Modal (%)			Dormant (%)		
	C.L.	IN	Both	C.L.	IN	Both	C.L.	IN	Both
Divorce/ Remarry									
1987	34	20	42	21	28	47	11	57	29
1993	35	23	38	23	37	39	12	56	30
Contra- ception									
1987	22	51	25	10	62	25	5	81	12
1993	23	46	28	12	57	28	7	70	20
Abortion									
1987	49	29	15	24	45	27	14	70	13
1993	35	31	31	19	45	32	9	56	35
Homo- sexual Behavior									
1987	47	27	16	30	37	23	17	65	12
1993	34	30	28	25	37	34	19	56	22
Extra- marital Sex									
1987	51	28	16	30	42	24	16	64	16
1993	39	36	24	21	42	33	12	57	28

Note: C.L. = Church leaders alone; IN = Individuals acting on consciences; Both = Church leaders and individuals together. Percent saying "Don't know" is not shown.

five issues did the Nuclears give more than 39 percent support to the option that church leaders alone should have the moral authority to decide rightness or wrongness.

As expected, the responses of the Modal and Dormant Catholics were even less supportive of the moral authority of the magisterium. On no item did more than one in four see church leaders as the sole source of moral authority. On all items the most frequent response was the individual, with a strong majority (61 percent) giving that response on birth control. Also, on all five items a larger percentage selected the laity working with church leaders than church leaders acting alone.

Figure 8.1
Nuclear Catholics: Percent Saying Final Moral Authority on Five Issues is with Church Leaders

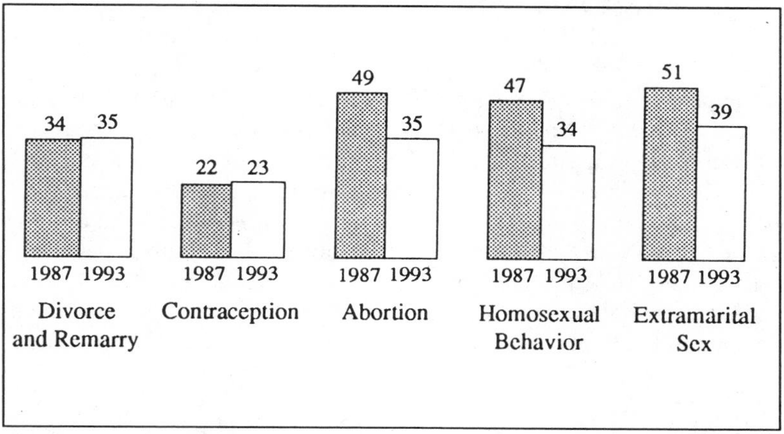

To summarize, in 1993 the Church's most highly committed joined the other Catholics in wanting more freedom to participate in decisions on issues involving morality than they now feel they have.

Attitudes toward Democratic Decision-Making

In Chapter 2, we discussed the laity's right to participate in Church decision-making and here we present further evidence of the desire for a greater role regardless of level of commitment (see Table 8.3). In both surveys a majority of the Nuclears said they favored more democratic decision-making in the parish, diocese and Vatican. By 1993 some 60 percent (Nuclear, Modal and Dormant) said they would like more democratic decision-making in Church affairs that do not

Table 8.3
Catholic Laity Favoring More Democratic Decision-Making, by Commitment, 1987 and 1993

	1987			1993		
	Nuclear (%)	Modal (%)	Dormant (%)	Nuclear (%)	Modal (%)	Dormant (%)
In parish	65	58	58	62	60	65
In diocese	62	54	49	63	58	59
Vatican	55	51	45	59	57	57

involve matters of faith than they have now. The movement toward consensus across all three categories is consistent with the earlier responses on the preferred locus of moral authority, and it reflects a trend examined by others (Bianchi & Ruether, 1992).

In 1987 and 1993 we asked our respondents to identify areas of church life in which they thought the laity should have the right to participate in making decisions (see Table 8.4). The first and perhaps most important finding has to do with the trends in responses between 1987 and 1993. In 1987 only one item elicited support from a majority of the Nuclears: how parish income should be spent. On matters such as birth control, divorce, assigning priests to parishes, and the ordination of women, the Nuclears favoring lay participation in decision-making ranged between 38 percent and 46 percent. In 1993 Nuclear majorities supported participation in all policy areas. As expected, strong majorities of Modal and Dormant Catholics favored lay participation in both surveys (see Table 8.4 and Figure 8.2).

The Church may not be a democracy, as many in the hierarchy are wont to remind the laity, but the reality is that the laity is taking a more active part in parish affairs in some dioceses, and laypersons are being called upon by bishops to administer priestless parishes, now numbering more than three hundred. So several forces seem to encourage the laity's enhanced roles. All three of our categories shifted in that direction between 1987 and 1993, not only the Catholics with a modest or weak commitment to the Church.

Table 8.4
Catholic Laity Supporting Right to Participate in Church Affairs, by Commitment, 1987 and 1993

	1987			1993		
	Nuclear (%)	Modal (%)	Dormant (%)	Nuclear (%)	Modal (%)	Dormant (%)
Parish Income	86	80	75	82	83	82
Select priests	46	60	67	60	75	88
Divorce policy	38	52	65	53	64	61
Birth control policy	41	53	70	55	64	63
Women priests	40	47	65	57	63	68

Figure 8.2
Nuclear Catholics: Percent Saying Laity Should Have the Right to Participate in Church Affairs

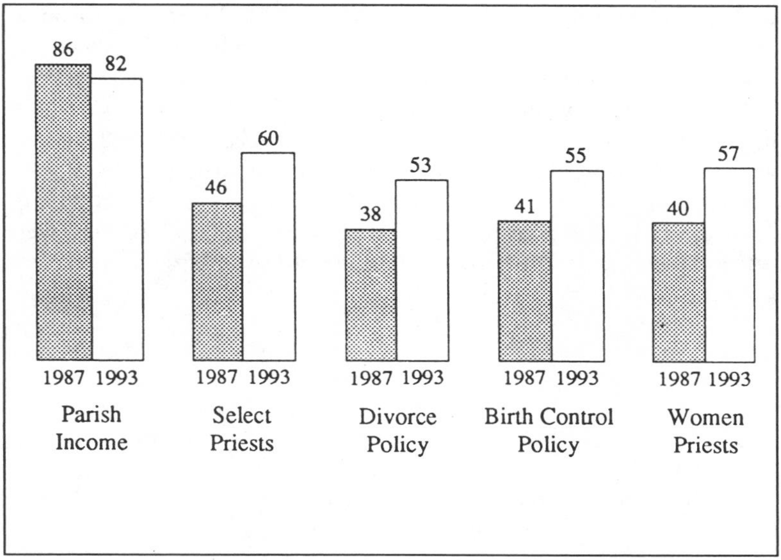

Being a Good Catholic

Among pre-Vatican II Catholics a set of norms helped define the good Catholic. Thus, among older Catholics at least, it has generally been accepted that a good Catholic attended Mass every week, obeyed the basic Church teachings, believed in the infallibility of the Pope, cared for the needy, and otherwise acted in accord with the norms. Our questions sought to probe the degree to which the image of the good Catholic was still held by the laity (see Table 8.5).

The strongest support for the traditional norms of the good Catholic was found among the Nuclears. Surprisingly, in both 1987 and 1993, about half of their number said that one could be a good Catholic without going to Mass weekly. This suprised us because after all, the Nuclears themselves were "regulars." Indeed, a significant proportion of the most-committed Catholics abandoned the traditional norms; even on abortion, 30 percent in 1993 said one could be a good Catholic and not obey the Church's teaching in that respect.

In both 1987 and 1993, but more so in 1993, the Modals and Dormants were consistent in their divergence from the traditional norms. This was so even on the matters of obedience to the Church's teaching on abortion and of belief in papal infallibility. Comparison of 1987 and 1993 reveals a definite trend away from traditional norms among Nuclears as well as the other two categories.

The finding on the question of donating time or money to help the poor is of some interest. The trend between 1987 and 1993 was for Nuclears, Modals and Dormants to say that one could be a good Catholic without doing so. Apparently, the Church's teachings are not having much effect in this area of social life either. This finding may well reflect the public's conflicted opinions about welfare, immigrants, and poverty.

Table 8.5
Catholic Lay Opinion on Whether a Person Can Be a Good Catholic by Commitment, 1987 and 1993

	1987			1993		
	Nuclear (%)	Modal (%)	Dormant (%)	Nuclear (%)	Modal (%)	Dormant (%)
Without attending Mass weekly	46	76	90	49	76	91
Without obeying birth control teaching	47	70	84	59	75	85
Without obeying abortion teaching	20	41	64	30	60	72
Without accepting papal infallibility	26	47	71	34	53	61
Without being married in the Church	35	46	48	46	53	56
Without helping the poor	38	46	48	46	53	56
Without contributing to Peter's Pence	57	69	84	71	79	88

The Priest Shortage

The questions about possible consequences of the shrinking priesthood were asked only in 1993:

> If a shortage of priests in the future required a reduction of priestly activities, some changes may occur in parish life. I am going to read a list of six changes which may occur. Please tell me after each if you would be willing to accept it in your home parish. Tell me if it would be very acceptable, somewhat acceptable, or not at all acceptable to you.

A majority of the Nuclears (see Table 8.6) said that three of our six possible changes would be acceptable: baptism by the laity (64 percent), no resident priest in the parish (61 percent), and no priests to visit the sick (51 percent). Nearly half (48 percent) said they would accept marriages performed by the laity, but only one in three found acceptable the lack of a priest to perform the last rites of the Church for the dying, and only 30 percent found acceptable reducing the number of Masses because of no priest to say them.

The same general patterns were found among the responses of the Modal and Dormant Catholics. Perhaps surprisingly, they were both less accepting of the lack of priests to visit the sick but more accepting of the possible reduction in Masses caused by a priest shortage. Both answers may make sense to these laypersons, who actually go to Mass much less often than do the Nuclears; they would find the availability of priests more meaningful at times of illness and near death.

Possible solutions to the priest shortage might be found in allowing married people to be priests or ordaining women priests. We asked

Table 8.6
Catholic Lay Acceptance of Possible Changes Ensuing from Priest Shortage, by Commitment, 1993

	1993		
	Nuclear (%)	Modal (%)	Dormant (%)
Deacon or lay Baptism	64	63	65
No resident priest	61	54	63
No priest to visit sick	51	40	32
Deacon or lay marriage	48	48	62
No priest for last rites	33	28	29
Reduce number of masses	30	42	51

about such possibilities in our last question. Only minorities among the three categories of laity accepted the argument that because the original leaders of the Church were men, the Church was bound not to waver from tradition; large majorities thought it would be good if married men were allowed to be priests, and large majorities (53 percent of the Nuclears) also said it would be good if the Church were to ordain women priests.

Discussion

In this chapter we have focused on the attitudes and beliefs of Nuclear Catholics, that is, those who by their own behavior and sense of self are the most highly committed. They attend Mass at least weekly, they hold the Church to be one of the most important features of their lives, and they say that they would never consider leaving the Church. It has often been argued that national surveys distort the degree to which the Catholic laity differs from the hierarchy on Church issues by including many Catholics who have only marginal ties to the Church. By use of our three measures of commitment we were able to separate the Nuclear Catholics from the Modal (those with moderate commitments) and Dormant (those with weak ties) Catholics.

One in four respondents was a Nuclear Catholic, in either the 1987 or 1993 survey. At the other extreme, fewer than one-fifth were identified as Dormant Catholics. In the six years between the two surveys, the Pope and the U.S. hierarchy took strong stands in support of traditional teachings on such issues as contraception, divorce and remarriage, abortion, homosexuality, non-marital sex, and a male-only, celibate clergy. Our surveys showed that the Nuclears were most likely of the three categories to have their commitment to the Church strengthened by the hierarchy's positions. At the same time, the size of this category did not grow as a result, and the percentage of Nuclears who were so strengthened did not grow.

One conclusion is inescapable: Nuclears shifted attitudes from 1987 to 1993 as much as Modals and Dormants did, and the shift moved them further from the hierarchy's teachings. It may be argued that the Church's efforts are important to sustain the attitudes and beliefs of the Nuclears in the face of changing societal norms and attitudes. Still, the data suggest that the Church's hold on the Nuclears has weakened over the period, most notably on the question dealing with the locus of moral authority. Statistically significant percentage declines in support of church teachings occurred relative to abortion, homosexuality, and non-marital sex. In fact, the Nuclears had the highest percentage changes among the three categories.

Further, the data on democratic participation in church affairs showed the Nuclears moving away from passive acceptance of church policy toward the position already held by the Modal and Dormant Catholics – that decision-making in the Church should not be circumscribed.

Finally, the Nuclears were the category most likely to find unacceptable the possible reduction of Masses on a regular basis. Because they were the ones most likely to be affected by such a curtailment, this finding is not surprising. And given the importance of weekly Masses to them, it is significant that they were as likely as the other Catholics to say that it would be a good thing if married men could be priests. And although they were less likely than the others to say so, a majority did support women's ordination.

The Nuclear Catholics represent the solid core, the rock upon which the future of the Church will be built, at least among the laity. But our demographic profile shows them to be older than the other Catholics, and predominantly female. In other parts of the book, we have shown that older people are more likely than younger to be traditional, and women, who have traditionally been the most stable element among the laity, are showing signs of change as dramatic as any.

To the extent the laity is important to the future of the institutional Church, these findings portend further troubles. Even if a significant number of Modal Catholics (who include many baby boomers) become Nuclear Catholics in the coming years, their commitment to the attitudes and beliefs that the leaders continue to insist upon is weak indeed.

References

Bianchi, Eugene C., and Rosemary Radford Ruether, eds. 1992. *A Democratic Catholic Church*. New York: Crossroad Press.

Fichter, Joseph H. 1951. *Southern Parish*. Chicago: University of Chicago Press.

________. 1954. *Social Relations in the Urban Parish*. Chicago: University of Chicago Press.

Hadaway, Kirk, Penny Long Marler, and Mark Chaves. 1993. "What the Polls Don't Show: A Closer Look at U.S. Church Attendance," *American Sociological Review*, 58 (December): 741-752.

Kosmin, Barry A., and Seymour P. Lachman. 1993. *One Nation Under God*. New York: Harmony Books.

Stark, Rodney, and William S. Bainbridge. 1985. *The Future of Religion*. Berkeley: University of California Press.

Woodward, Kenneth. 1993. "The Rites of Americans," *Newsweek*, 29 November: 80-82.

9

Latinos and First-Wave Catholics: Are They Different?

OUR PURPOSE IN THIS CHAPTER IS TO PRESENT A DEMOGRAPHIC SKETCH of the Catholic Latino population that was included in our survey of Spring 1993, and then to compare the responses of the Latinos to those of the sample as a whole (made up mostly of first-wave Catholics, those who migrated to the United States from Europe during the nineteenth and early twentieth centuries). Fifteen percent of the 1993 sample was of Latino background, and was represented in all four regions of the country. The Bureau of the Census reported the following distribution of the Hispanic-origin population in 1989: California, 34 percent; Texas, 21 percent; New York, 10 percent; Florida, 8 percent; New Mexico, 8 percent; Illinois, 4 percent; and other, 15 percent. Thus, our sample seems to be fairly representative of the national distribution, including Puerto Ricans, Cubans, Mexican Americans, and other Central and South Americans.

The American bishops have estimated that some 85 percent of Latinos in the United States are Roman Catholic; Gallup and other polls suggest that the figure may be closer to 65 percent or 70 percent (Schoenherr and Young, 1993:300; Kosmin and Lachman, 1993:138). Whatever the number, there is no doubt about two things: Protestant churches are actively recruiting Latinos in the religious marketplace, and the Latino population will continue to grow faster than the rest of the Catholic population in the coming decade. The Bureau of the Census estimates that the Latino population is growing about five times as fast as the rest of the population, and that this has been true since 1980. Immigration accounts for half the gain (Schoenherr and Young, 1993:299). Projections are that another eight million Latinos will be added to the U.S. population by the year 2005. Whether they will be Catholic, Protestant, or unchurched is a question, but the data available are instructive.

Schoenherr and Young (1993:299-300) estimate that some ten to twelve million Latinos in the United States are marginal Catholics at best. If the Church is serious about its evangelizing mission, this seems an obvious opportunity for an all-out effort. For example, Kosmin and Lachman (1993:138-139) found that only 52 percent of Puerto Rican-origin 1990 high school seniors identified themselves as Roman Catholics; 53.8 percent of Central- and South American-origin high school seniors also so identified themselves. Even among Mexican-origin high school seniors the percentage Catholic was only 59 percent.

Among the most pressing problems facing Church leaders is the shortage of Latino priests, who constitute only four percent of the national total of priests, whereas "Hispanic Catholic believers are 14 percent of all U.S. Catholics" (Kosmin and Lachman, 1993: 139). About three times as many Latinos are currently enrolled in Protestant seminaries and schools of theology as in Catholic seminaries. Kosmin and Lachman attribute part of this trend to the fact that the Protestants place less emphasis on academic requirements than do the Catholics and more emphasis on spiritual anointing.

Figure 9.1
U.S. Hispanic Population, by Type, 1988

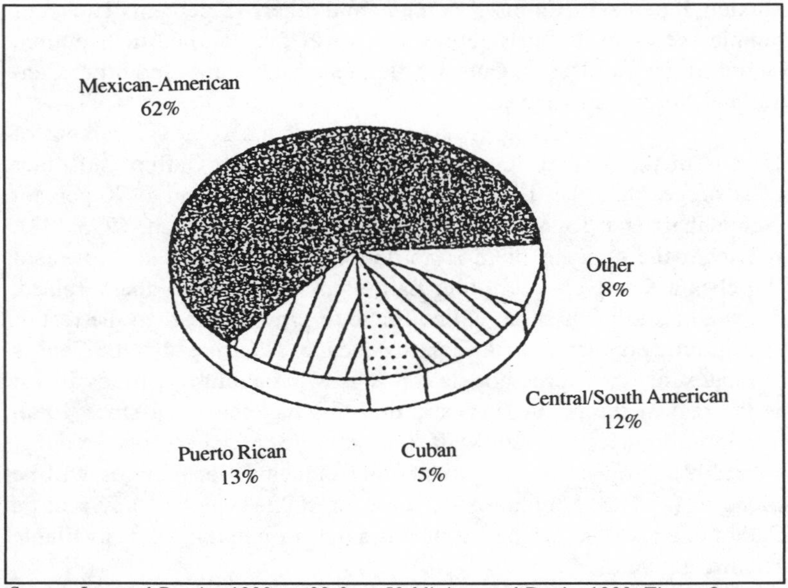

Source: Lee and Potvin, 1992, p. 33 from Valdivieso and Davis, 1988, Figure 2.

The Latinos: A Demographic Sketch

The 1990 Census reported 22.4 million Latinos, or nine percent of the total U.S. population of 249 million (Lee and Potvin, 1992:37-39). That was an increase of eight million over the 1980 count, and did not include the undercount, mainly of undocumented aliens, who may be as many as another three or four million. Figure 9.1 shows the percentage of each major ethnic group of Latinos in the United States, and figure 9.2 shows their general distribution.

Figure 9.2
Total Hispanic Population, by Region and State with 500,000 or More

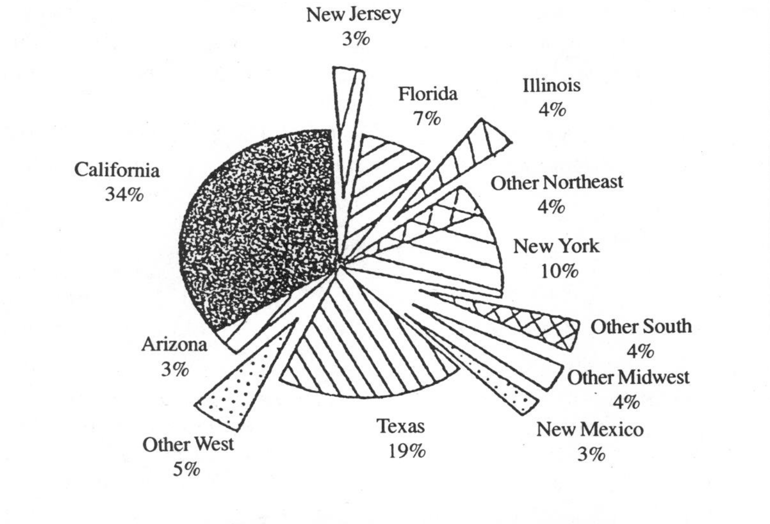

Source: U.S. Bureau of Census 1991; cited in Lee and Potvin, 1992 p. 34.

According to Deck (1989:9-12) about one half of the Latinos are below the age of 25; for the United States as a whole, the median age is 31.9. And, some 28.7 percent of Latino families consist of five persons or more; the same is true for only 14.9 percent of the United States as a whole. Persons of Mexican origin are about 60 percent of the U.S. Latino population. Some 88 percent of all Latinos live in urban areas, more than 50 percent in inner cities, with one in four living below the poverty level. Some 57 percent have no high school diploma;

79 percent are blue-collar workers, and only six percent are still in agriculture.

About 10 percent of the Latinos have completed college (Lee and Potvin, 1992:47), yet Latinos have the lowest high school completion rate (under 60 percent throughout the 1980s) among persons ages 20 to 24. Blacks have reached the 80 percent level, and whites the 90 percent level (p. 45). In 1993 the Department of Education reported that the drop-out rate among Latinos was 27.5 percent; for the 16-24 age group as a whole, the rate was 11 percent (*Washington Post,* 1994). On the other hand, the vast majority in the second generation are bilingual, with 90 percent proficient in English. Indeed, in the third generation, more than half speak English only (Deck, 1989:12).

Cubans, the smallest group of Latinos in the United States, have the highest education, occupation, and income levels, the lowest fertility, and the lowest rates of dropping their Catholic identity (Lee and Potvin, 1992: 43).

Our 1993 survey data represent Latinos who have telephones and use English well enough to participate in a Gallup survey.

Latinos and American Society

Peter Steinfels (1994) offers the following observation about the way the Catholic Church melds newcomers with old-timers into its parishes:

> Few other American institutions stretch as effectively across lines of ethnicity, race, education and economic class as the Catholic Church. However tenuously, the Church links outsiders like St. Thomas' new immigrants with the college-educated grandchildren of Irish, Italian and Slavic immigrants, now insiders occupying city halls and downtown executive suites.

Although on the surface the embrace of the Church seems to be a hopeful sign of social support for the new immigrants, the situation is much less certain. Latino religious leaders have expressed great concern about the socialization process in the United States and its possible impact on the Latino population. For example, the Jesuit priest Allan Figueroa Deck, who has been especially active in the Hispanic ministry, has written extensively on the dilemmas and dangers facing Latino culture as Latinos become socialized into the ways of American society.

The North American culture is seen by Deck (1989:xv, xvi) as "materialistic, individualistic, and hedonistic." The danger is that Latinos evangelized into the Catholic Church in the United States will become evangelized also into the American culture. Deck says that it is hard to find the Gospel values in American culture, or even in American Roman Catholicism. It is especially worrisome to him that Latinos seem likely to be poor for a significant period, longer than the European first-wave Catholics were poor. The poverty threatens to combine with an exaggerated individualism and commercialism to destroy the Latino heritage without instilling a new sense of Gospel values.

Further, Deck (1989:3) notes that the internal crisis caused by the decline in vocations to the priesthood portends severe problems for the church in the United States. But here an important distinction must be made. There is a great difference between the church in the U.S. and the church to which Latinos are accustomed in the role played by the clergy and the parochial schools: the United States has a much more clerical church, one not as familiar to the Latinos. But, so far, the outreach of the first wave to the second wave has been lackluster.

In 1987 the American bishops instituted a national pastoral plan for the Latinos, including the ambitious Base Ecclesial Communities Project, which has an office in Washington, D.C., and a lay administrator. But in many ways their actions have not matched their words up to now.[1] And sexual abuse scandals in the Southwest, mixed with ambivalent and ambiguous support for migrant workers in California, have further clouded the picture.

Deck is quick to admit that U.S. society embodies noble values, such as democracy, egalitarianism, personal autonomy, and women's rights. The problem for both the first and second waves is to seek for the relevance of Christ's Gospel in their two respective cultures, and bring them together in an enriched synthesis. The danger is that the worst elements of American culture will overwhelm the Gospel message and Deck (1989:19) acknowledges the challenge: "While cultural pluralism is a real choice for Latinos, the greater reality is that historical experience and patterns show something else happening in the long run; namely, the *de facto* Americanization of ethnic groups."

The foregoing serves as background for a demographic profile taken from the Catholics Speak Out (CSO) survey and our 1993 survey (see Table 9.1).

---

1. For an insider's view of the impact of Puerto Rican Migration upon the Archdiocese of New York, see *Oxcart Catholicism on Fifth Avenue,* by Ana Maria Diaz-Stevens, University of Notre Dame Press, 1993.

Table 9.1
Demographic Characteristics,
First-Wave and Latino Catholics, 1993

	Total (%)	FWC (%)	Latino (%)
Education			
Less than high school	20	16	46
High school graduate	39	40	30
Some college	21	22	15
College graduate	13	14	6
Grad/prof. school	8	8	4
Catholic Education			
Grade school	51	55	27
High school	24	26	4
College	8	9	4
Annual Income			
Less than $10,000	18	16	26
$10,000-19,999	23	20	38
$20,000-29,999	20	20	14
$30,000-39,999	17	19	9
$40,000-49,999	9	9	8
$50,000+	15	16	5
Sex			
Male	48	49	42
Female	52	51	58
Age			
18-29	27	25	35
30-39	25	26	23
40-54	23	24	19
55+	25	25	24
Region			
East	37	41	15
Midwest	22	20	33
South	23	26	5
West	18	14	48

Our sample showed that 46 percent of Latinos had no high school diploma (57 percent was reported by Deck for 1985). Ten percent of the Latinos had at least a college degree; this was true for 22 percent of the other respondents. More than half of the latter had a parochial school education, compared with 27 percent for the Latinos; the discrepancy was more remarkable at the high school level. Our Latino sample had a somewhat greater proportion of women (58 percent) than the sample as a whole (51 percent), and Latinos were more likely than the others to be under age 30. (Recall from census data that half of the Latino population was under age 25.) Two-thirds of the Latinos in our study reported family incomes under $20,000 a year; the same was true for only one-third of the first-wave Catholics. At the other end of the income scale, first-wave Catholics were twice as likely as the Latinos to have incomes of $30,000 or more. And finally, a word about the regional distribution of the Latinos: almost half of our sample came from the West and our figures for the Midwest and East also correspond well with the census-reported distribution.

In sum, the demographic picture derived from our sample fits with the national data: Latinos are younger; have much less formal education and less Catholic education; for the most part, earn less; have a higher proportion of females; and are closely reflective of the regions of the country in which they are more numerous.

Latinos and Moral Authority

Are Latinos more or less like the first-wave Catholics in their attitudes and behavior relative to a range of official church teachings? We compared the views of first-wave Catholics (FWCs) and Latinos on questions about church moral authority. First, do the two groups differ about who should have the final say on what is right and wrong? In the Catholic press we have sometimes read that Latinos are more conservative than FWCs on Catholic issues.

In Chapter 2 we saw that Catholic-community attitudes as a whole are shifting from reliance on church teachings to the view that church leaders and laity need to work together on moral issues. In the 1993 survey the Latinos and first-wave Catholics were similar in not looking to church leaders to determine the morality of a set of items. Only with regard to divorce and remarriage without an annulment and homosexual relationships did as many as 29 percent of Latinos say that the locus of moral authority should rest with church leaders alone. The Latinos were actually even more in favor than the FWCs of church leaders and the laity's working together, or on individual consciences alone (the latter was more often the modal response of the FWCs). For example, on decisions concerning a Catholic's "practicing contraceptive birth control," 46 percent of the Latinos favored collaboration compared with 23 percent of the FWCs; concerning "sex relations outside marriage," 47 percent of the Latinos and 28 percent of the FWCs; concerning a Catholic's "advocating free choice regarding abortion," 49 percent of the Latinos and 30 percent of the FWCs.

Table 9.2
Attitudes of First-Wave and Latino Catholics to Democratic Decision-Making

Q: Some people think the Catholic Church should have more democratic decision-making in Church affairs that do not involve matters of faith than it has at the present time. Do you favor or oppose this idea. . .

	Favor	
	FWCs (%)	Latinos (%)
At the parish level?	64	47
At the diocesan level?	61	59
At the level of the Vatican?	58	54

Are the views of Latinos different on whether laity should have the right to participate in decision-making? No. They are similar to those of FWCs on issues like whether laity should help select priests for parishes; whether laity should have a role in making church policy on divorce and birth control, and similar matters.

Are Latinos more, or less, in favor of more democratic decision-making in Church affairs (that is, affairs not involving matters of faith) than are FWCs? In the 1993 survey, Latinos were less inclined to favor democratic procedures than were the FWCs, and less in favor at the *parish* level than at the level of the *Vatican* (see Table 9.2). The difference between the Latinos and first-wave Catholics was significant at the parish and diocesan levels, with more than 60 percent of the latter favoring more democracy in those two situations.

We also asked if the American Catholic Church should become more or less independent of the Vatican; on this the Latinos and FWCs agreed closely. The 1992 survey asked about several possible changes in parish structures to make them more participative, for example, if "parishioners should be able to choose their own pastors." There the Latinos and FWCs were in general agreement as well in that most looked upon the proposals positively.

The first-wave Catholics and Latinos, then, did not differ greatly on these topics. The Latinos were more inclined to endorse a participative Church in some respects, less inclined in others. On balance, they were a bit less in favor of institutional change than the earlier arrivers but not much so. And this circumstance may well reflect their sense of priorities and concerns. The questions asked may not have dealt with what are the central issues in Roman Catholicism for them. Still, the Latino responses carried the values of democracy, freedom, and autonomy that Deck (1989) pointed to as positive features of American society.

Educational Differences among Latinos

We have already noted the lower levels of educational achievement among the Latinos, levels that reflect their primarily first- and second-generation status. We can expect educational levels to continue to rise as more and more achieve third- and fourth-generation status. We looked at the differences between the FWCs and Latino Catholics in both our 1993 survey and the 1992 survey and those we found were weak and mixed. For example, the first-wave and Latino responses were similar on whether one could be a good Catholic without going to Mass every weekend and without complying with a range of other heretofore customary church expectations. The Latinos with less than a high school diploma were at least as likely as first-wave Catholics to say yes to all nine items. The same held for the Latinos compared with the FWCs who had at least some college education. Indeed, on two items, helping the poor and helping the parish, the Latino responses were significantly more supportive.

Some 43 percent of first-wave Catholics regardless of educational level said the Church was one of the most important influences on their lives; among the Latinos, 41 percent of those with less than a high school education said this, but only 34 percent of those with some college. And although education was not a predictor of weekly Mass attendance among the FWCs, it did appear to have some effect on the Latinos; those with at least some college reported more Mass attendance than did the other Latinos. Thus, the limited evidence suggests that the effect of education on Latinos will resemble its effect on other Catholics.

The Church's Most-Committed Latinos

In Chapter 8 we categorized Catholics by degree of commitment to the Church. The most highly committed (Nuclear Catholics) were those who said that they went to Mass at least weekly, that the Church was one of the most important influences in their lives, and that they would never leave the Church.[2] The nuclears constituted 23 percent of the 1993 sample. Of the Latino portion of our 1993 sample, only 11 percent can be described as highly committed by these three indicators. Fifty-six percent of the first-wave Catholics were Modal Catholics (they went to Mass at least monthly, said the Church was an important force in their lives, and said they would probably never leave); of the Latinos 67 percent fell into that category.

Finally, 21 percent of the FWCs and 22 percent of the Latinos were Dormant (very low commitment). The latter figure is much lower than other studies have reported; Kosmin and Lachman (1993), Deck (1989), and Lee and Potvin (1993) describe as many as half of all Latino Catholics marginal or dormant.

The Age Factor among First-Wave and Latino Catholics

Because of our small sample, we compared the first-wave and Latino Catholics by dividing the respondents into those who were 40 years old or older and those who were under 40.

The most obvious finding is that there were few if any differences between the first-wave and Latino Catholics on many items, and only small differences on others. For example, there were no meaningful differences on items relating to commitment to the parish, level of confidence in the bishops, confidence in the Vatican, and knowledge of the peace and economic pastorals; nor any on whether the American bishops should be more independent of the Vatican; nor any by age, on what it takes to be a good Catholic.

Differences that are worth noting may be summarized as follows:

1. Controlling for age, ethnicity affected the way young Catholics reacted to issues such as birth control, abortion, and reports of homosexuality among priests. On four of the five issues we looked at, the first-wave Catholics under 40 were considerably more likely

2. The reader will recall that we created a 7-point scale with point 1 being "I would never leave the Catholic Church," and point 7 being "Yes, I might leave the Catholic Church." In most cases, we combined points 1 and 2 as the indicator that they would never leave the Catholic Church. In the present instance, points 1 and 2 were used.

than young Latinos to say these issues had weakened their faith. For example, 46 percent of the young FWCs said the Church teaching on birth control had caused a weakening of their commitment; only 15 percent of the young Latino Catholics said so. Similarly, 41 percent of the young FWCs said priests' homosexuality had weakened their faith; only 29 percent of the young Latino Catholics said so. The one item on which there was no significant difference concerned the ordination of women.

Divergence between the two groups' older components was smaller. On only two items were differences as great as 10 percentage points. The older Latino Catholics were twice as likely (33 percent to 16 percent) to say that the church teaching on abortion had weakened their faith, and more likely (39 percent to 29 percent) to say that reports of homosexuality among priests had weakened their faith.

2. Ethnicity also affected the way our respondents thought about authority and democracy in the Church. The Latinos were more inclined than first-wave Catholics to say that Church officials and lay people should share responsibility for policies relating to issues such as birth control, abortion, and sex outside marriage. The FWCs were more inclined to say individual laypeople should have the final say on such matters. This pattern was similar to the samples discussed in more general terms above.

3. The young FWCs were more likely than the young Latino Catholics to say they preferred more democracy at all levels of Church life. For example, 70 percent of the former compared with 48 percent of the latter said they wanted more democracy in their parishes; at the diocesan level, 66 percent and 49 percent. Again, 86 percent of the young FWCs and 71 percent of the young Latino Catholics favored more lay involvement in decisions on how parish income is spent. On matters like birth control, the young FWCs were more disposed toward lay participation in making those decisions: 66 percent to 54 percent.

   The older Latino Catholics were different from the older FWCs in favoring more lay participation in decisions having to do with priest selection (76 percent to 64 percent), and birth control (72 percent to 58 percent). However, the older Latinos were less likely than their FWC peers to lean toward lay participation in decisions about the ordination of women (42 percent to 57 percent).

5. The older Latino Catholics were more likely than the FWCs to say that the Church was important to them (55 percent to 43 percent), but Mass attendance rates were about the same. The older Latinos also said they prayed more often (83 percent daily to 66 percent).

6. The young Latinos were more likely than the young FWCs (63 percent to 48 percent) to say they would never leave the Church.

7. The only area in which the FWCs seemed more traditional had to do with accommodations to the priest shortage. Regardless of age, they were more likely to say that adjustments to the priest shortage were unacceptable. The Latinos seemed to be more willing to "bend to the wind."

Human Sexuality

There were areas of agreement and disagreement between first-wave Catholics and Latino Catholics on a range of questions dealing with human sexuality. The differences and the similarities are striking. For example, the two groups were alike (13 percent and 14 percent respectively) in the small percentage saying that abortion should never be legal. At the other end, 29 percent of FWCs and 36 percent of the Latinos said that abortion should be legal in all circumstances.

Regarding the morality of abortion, again only a small minority (13 percent and 12 percent) said it could never be a morally acceptable choice, with a small minority saying it could always be a morally acceptable choice. In this connection, the modal response (41 percent and 45 percent) was that it could be a morally acceptable choice only in rare instances.

In most instances relating to sexual behavior, the differences between the two groups were small. On contraceptive birth control, 89 percent of FWCs and 79 percent of Latinos said the Church should permit it. And again the FWCs were much more likely (78 percent to 59 percent) to say that divorced and remarried Catholics should be full Church members. On the use of condoms, premarital sex and gay sex, the two groups were again pretty much in concert. Given the differences in educational levels, and given our knowledge that as educational levels go up, Latino responses to questions on such matters will move in the direction of those of the FWCs, it seems clear that on these, as on the other topics discussed, Latino Catholics are not likely to be different from other Catholics in the future.

The Gender Factor

The Latino men tended to mirror the FWC men in our sample on commitment indicators like "never leaving the Church" and Mass attendance, but they were less likely to say that the Church is the most or among the most important parts of their lives (23 percent and 37 percent). The Latino women mirrored the FWC women on the importance of the Church in their lives, but they were much higher than the FWCs on two measures of commitment: 71 percent would never leave the church, compared with 56 percent,[3] and 67 percent said they attended Mass at least weekly, compared with 43 percent.

The Latino men were very similar to first-wave men regarding lay participation in deciding about women's ordination, and in agreeing that it would be a good thing if women were allowed to be ordained priests. However only 3 percent of the Latino men compared with 16 percent of the FWC men said that the policy of ordaining men, but not women, strengthened their commitment to the Church. The Latino women, on the other hand, were very similar to all the FWC women on the question of participating in decisions regarding women's ordination and on saying that the policy of ordaining men, but not women strengthened their commitment. On the other hand, they were much less likely to say that it would be good if women were ordained priests; 41 percent agreed, compared with 61 percent of the FWC women.

On birth control and abortion, the Latino men and women mirrored the general sample on all but one aspect. A minority of the Latino men (45 percent) said that the laity should participate in making Church policy on birth control, compared to 58 percent of the first-wave men. At the same time, the gender factor is strong on this issue: 74 percent of the Latino women said the laity should have the right to participate in making Church policy on birth control.

The Latino men and women were similar to their first-wave counterparts in agreeing that a person can be a good Catholic without obeying the Church teachings on divorce and remarriage. However, only 42 percent of Latino men said one can be a good Catholic without getting married in the Church, as against 59 percent of the first-wave men. The gender difference is again significant: 77 percent of the Latino women said yes on this item. In fact, the Latino women were more likely to say yes than were the first-wave women (64 percent). Almost the same pattern obtained when it came to participation in making Church policy on divorce: only 40 percent of the Latino men said laypeople should have the right, compared with 53 percent of the first-wave men; and more than three-fourths of the Latino women said so, compared with two-thirds of first-wave women.

On questions dealing with parish changes and the priest shortage, the Latino women and men also mirrored the sample, with one exception. The Latino women were much less likely than the first-wave

---

3. In this instance we included only those whose responses were at point 1 on the 7-point scale.

women (26 percent and 39 percent) to accept the situation of no resident priest but only a lay administrator and visiting priests in the parish. The gender difference is even stronger; 47 percent of the Latino men said they would accept the situation.

Summary

To summarize, Latino Catholics differ significantly from first-wave Catholics on a number of important demographic variables. And they bring to American Catholicism a Catholicism much more rooted in family than in the institutional Church. At the same time, their orientation to the range of sexuality and marriage issues that have occupied so much of church news in recent years is fairly close to that of the American Catholic laity in general. On matters of authority and governance, their responses are again similar to those of first-wave Catholics.

Overall, the findings lend little or no support to the notion that Latino Catholics are different from other Catholics in their opposition to the magisterium's teachings on the major sexuality issues of our time. Our most reasonable guess is that they will come to resemble first-wave Catholics even more as time goes on.

References

Deck, Allan Figueroa. 1989. *The Second Wave: Hispanic Ministry and the Evangelization of Cultures*. New York: Paulist Press.

Diaz Stevens, Ana Maria. 1993. *Oxcart Catholicism on Fifth Avenue*. South Bend: University of Notre Dame Press.

Kosmin, Barry A., and Seymour P. Lachman. 1993. *One Nation Under God*. New York: Harmony Books.

Lee, Che-Fu, and Raymond H. Potvin. 1993. "A Demographic Profile of U.S. Hispanics" In *Strangers and Aliens No More*. Washington, D.C.: NCCB/USCC Office of Research.

Schoenherr, Richard A., and Lawrence A. Young. 1993. *Full Pews and Empty Altars*. Madison: University of Wisconsin Press.

Steinfels, Peter. 1994. "Ancient Rock in Crosscurrents of Today." *New York Times*. 29 May: 1-20.

Valdivieso, R., and C. Davis. 1988. "U.S. Hispanics: Challenging Issues for 1990s." A publication of the Population Reference Bureau, Inc. no. 17 (December).

The Washington Post. 1994. 15 September: A14.

10

Future Directions in American Catholicism

IN THE MIDST OF ALL THE ENERGY, NOISE, AND DIVERSITY OF AMERICAN Catholic life, sociology as an academic discipline can make a contribution. Careful sociological research helps the observer step back a bit from the headlines and examine underlying cultural changes. The changes are slow but have momentous influence on the future. The research we have presented is painstaking in its measurement and display of underlying trends not noticed in day-to-day activity.

In Chapter 1 we documented an historic tension within the American Catholic Church: a struggle between Catholics who want their Church to be integrated into American society and want the Church to affirm American culture, and those that want the Church to reaffirm its European traditions, and even be a countercultural force in American society. Like Greeley (1967:22) we believe "the struggle over which of these options ought to be followed has been the single most important theme of American Catholic history." The late 19th-century trend toward integration was followed by an early-20th-century trend toward the restoration of European traditions (Dolan: 1985). This was followed by a clear movement toward integration, inspired by the papacy of John XXIII and Vatican II.

Examining the scene in 1967, Greeley concluded that "In theory, the Americanizers have carried the day. But, . . . in practice, the victory of the Americanizers has been anything but complete. Ecclesiastical policy as distinguished from ecclesiastical theory has frequently been of the anti-Americanizing variety" (pp. 20-21). He foresaw that if the hierarchy insisted on an anti-American stance, "Catholicism would be in for difficult times in the years to come" (p. 21).

The events of recent years have supported Greeley's analysis, as tensions have again risen. On one side, integrationist groups like Call To Action have called for the implementation of the documents of Vatican II and other democratic reforms, while on the other side restorationist groups like Catholics United for the Faith have rallied in support of hierarchy and papal supremacy. Our study of the American Catholic laity has focused on several issues which reflect the integration-restoration struggle.

The Trend Toward Integration

The lesson of the book is clear: a majority of the American Catholic laity is slowly moving in the direction of wanting a more democratic Church in which laypersons can participate at all levels. This desire is strengthening with the passage of time, according to the research reported in this book. In the chapters on authority, human sexuality, changes across three generations, the role of women, post-Vatican II Catholics, the Church's most committed, and Latino Catholics, we have seen how growing numbers of the laity have been abandoning the traditional positions demanded by the magisterium.

Even as they urge more democratic decision-making at all levels of Church structure, the ordination of women, the reactivation of married priests, and a more nuanced sexual morality, only a small minority of all Catholics (less than 20 percent) said they were thinking of leaving the Church. They insist they are a part of the people of God, that this is their church too, and that it can and must be reformed.

What is causing the call for reform? We lack clear-cut statistical proof, but we believe that several influences are foremost. American Catholics today are more highly educated than ever, more at ease as full participants in the exercise of social and political power from Congress to boardroom, more often in contact with other Christian religious groups, and more in tune with American ideals of individual freedom, personal autonomy, and democracy. American Catholics have become American – in every way. They are now solidly in the mainstream of American society politically, socially, and economically. The situation today is a culmination of a half century of constant change.

Advocates of the European restoration vision are critical of these changes, much more inclined to defend traditional Church structures and teachings as a necessary bulwark against the society, and critical of Vatican II. They see modern life as decadent, evidenced by the prevalence of nonmarital sex, use of contraceptives, remarriage after divorce, and abortions.[1] They see little that is redeeming in the overall

---

1. The recent book *The Social Organization of Sexuality*, by Laumann *et al*, suggests that Americans are much more conservative in their sexual practices, faithful to their spouses, and satisfied with their sex lives, than restorationists want to believe. Laumann

culture and argue that the Church needs to become a counterculture. Above all, it needs to maintain its institutional structures and authority intact. If this means a smaller, less-all-accepting church in the future, that may not be too great a price to pay. Our findings show that only a minority of Catholics support much or all of the restorationist position. But it is a strong, articulate, and highly committed minority, and on issues like abortion it has proven highly effective in the public realm.

To help us recognize the extent of the changes that have taken place, let us review briefly some of the key findings. The following examples typify these findings. For sake of convenience, we can group these findings under three major headings: the Church's mode of governance; issues involving parish life; and a range of issues involving sexual morality.

In Chapter 2 and elsewhere, we found that on the question of the mode of governance, a growing majority of Catholics rejected the idea that church leaders alone should be deciding what is or is not moral in a range of issues broadly defined as sexual morality. Age, gender, ethnicity and level of commitment had some impact, but the trend remained clear: over the six year period of the two studies, Catholics of all categories moved away from the restorationist and toward the integrationist position. Only among the Church's most committed (Nuclear Catholics) did as many as 40 percent identify church leaders alone as the proper source for determining the morality of sexual issues (Table 8.2).

On a range of questions dealing with the right to participate in decisions regarding Church roles and parish life (see especially Chapters 2, 6 and 7), they again expressed their strong belief in the right to participate. One of the more noteworthy changes in six years was the increase in the percentages of women supporting the statement that the laity should have the right to participate in deciding whether women should be ordained to the priesthood. The increase was from 45 percent in 1987 to 65 percent in 1993 (Table 6.2).

Finally, as an example of the way the laity view the Church's teachings on matters of sexual morality, we note that even on abortion, an issue that the bishops and the pope have spoken on so often in recent years, and an issue that is politically divisive in American society, a growing number of laity distance themselves from the official teach-

---

et al make clear that there has been a revolution in attitudes toward sex, including especially the finding that only 20 percent of the population 18-59 said that pre-marital sex was always wrong, while 48 percent said it was not wrong at all.

ings. Only 13 percent of all Catholics, and 22 percent of the weekly Mass attenders said that abortion should be illegal in all circumstances (Table 3.2).

What if we dislike the trends we see? Can we turn back? Trends such as we have documented here are not easily stopped, much less reversed. Can the movement toward individual autonomy among Catholic laity be reversed? Can the women's movements of the last three decades be reversed? Can the lay activities in parishes be stopped? Can the inquiring questions of young Catholics be silenced? We cannot imagine how! Especially since these trends are grounded in the documents and spirit of Vatican II, as well as in the ethos of American society.

The conclusion is stark: the *status quo ante* is fading. Responsible Church leaders, clergy and lay, need to prepare thoughtfully now for the future.

If we convince the reader that trends are in motion, that they are strong, and that they have an inherent momentum, it is enough for one book. The only thing more we can do here is to add some commentary and clarify prospects in the hope of upgrading discussions about what should be done.

Supporting Evidence from Other Research

Our understanding of present-day trends and our belief that the integrationist vision is the more realistic are shared by other researchers. Patrick McNamara (1992:158) carried out a study of graduates of a suburban middle-class Catholic high school in the Southwest and found that only one-third said that their Catholicism was basically the same as their parents'. A large majority were no longer attending Mass regularly or adhering to the Church's moral teachings. For the majority of young Catholics, "being Catholic is not that compelling or formative of ideals or viewpoints." Rather, young Catholics are seeking a "teaching authority that is both rational and reasonable . . . . These young men and women find congenial the respectful approach of their teachers that acknowledges their own thinking and experiences" (p. 159). They defended the right to think for themselves and wished that the Church would honor this right. The young adults in our book felt the same way.

In *Holy Siege*, Kenneth Briggs (1992) provides an in-depth account of fourteen months of conflict, confusion, and change in the American Catholic Church in order to depict the underlying cultural shifts as they play out in event after event. The account begins with the Vatican's 1986 decision to withdraw Father Charles Curran's right to teach as a Catholic theologian in the Catholic University and ends with Pope John Paul II celebrating Mass in the Pontiac Silverdome in 1987. Briggs shows how laity, clergy, and hierarchy struggled between the opposing forces. His case studies add depth to our findings.

A different approach to the present-day struggle can be found in Gene Burns' *The Frontiers of Catholicism* (1992). He provides historical depth and insight into the Europeanist versus Americanist struggle of the late nineteenth century. Burns argues that the loss of the Papal States, and thus of the centuries-old temporal power of the Vatican, led it to seek control of the minds and consciences of the laity concerning moral issues. On sociopolitical issues, the magisterium would issue encyclicals from time to time, e.g. *Rerum Novarum*, but they would be general in nature and not binding on anyone's conscience.

In our time the Vatican has attempted to make abortion a moral issue instead of a sociopolitical issue. Burns warns that the abortion issue is testing the American Catholic hierarchy's ability to maintain its moral authority with Catholics on social issues, as increasing numbers of lay people move in the integrationist direction.

Our findings suggest that as Catholics have learned to read the social encyclicals and pastoral letters of the bishops as nothing more than moral guidance not binding in conscience, they have felt free to debate and criticize them as they did for example with the economy pastoral in the 1980s. This may help explain why the Vatican has been unable to win their consciences on the issue of abortion. So too have the laity begun to question the magisterium's moral teachings on private life that are supposed to be binding in conscience.

It is true as Burns reminds us that the laity is the least powerful segment of the Roman Catholic Church. But it is also true that Vatican II and American culture provide a great degree of personal freedom to the laity. Our surveys raise the question of whether and how the Church can control the laity if the laity is more and more immune to the Church's traditional claimed authority.

We have already alluded several times to Greeley's 1967 study of *The Catholic Experience*, and of how his analysis anticipated the present tensions. In *Faithful Attraction* (1991) Greeley provides important empirical findings on sexuality and marriage. In his research he finds that American marriages are generally happy, most couples are faithful to their partners, and American couples enjoy sex. This is true for Catholics as well as others; that is, they are not wandering off into immoral or unstable behavior when they follow their own judgments and experience on matters like use of contraceptives, *in vitro* fertilization, divorce and remarriage. They are doing very well, thank you. Greeley adds that "those who wish to reassert the traditional premarital norms will accomplish nothing by denouncing premarital sex as immoral. The audience no longer agrees" (p. 204).

Finally, Richard Schoenherr and Lawrence Young's *Full Pews and Empty Altars* (1993) looks at trends in the recruitment, ordination and retention of clergy. They describe the decline in numbers of priests and project a future in which the shortage will precipitate a crisis. It will bring changes at the parish level threatening the weekly celebration of the Mass, which is the core of Catholic worship. More and more of the laity will be denied the most basic of priestly services, that is, adequate access to the Eucharist celebration, unless married men and women are allowed to be ordained, policies which increasing numbers of lay people are inclined to favor.

To sum up: the findings in our study do not stand alone. They are consonant with other research conclusions in the past few years. Some version of the American integrationist outcome is the most probable future of the Catholic Church in the United States in the next two decades.

The Integrationist Trajectory

What does the integrationist trajectory look like? The Church will gradually include more laypersons in decision-making at all levels, from parish to diocese to Vatican.[2] The laity will demand more say in selection of priests and even bishops. Parishes will have more and more lay professional staff, and increasing numbers of parishes will be led entirely by laypersons (often religious sisters) because of the shortage of ordained priests. All levels of the Church will be forced into open accountability in financial matters and the use of advisory committees (including laypersons) at all budgeting levels. Theological definitions of *priesthood* and *lay status* will be open to modification. The centralized power of the Church in the Vatican will come under pressure in favor of a more federated Church structure.[3]

---

2. We have documented some of the evidence on lay participation in the chapter on the future of the parish. Murnion (1992) reported that more than 20,000 lay people now work in administrative posts within the institutional Church, and the number will grow in the years ahead. The interested reader should see also two Sheed & Ward publications, *Working in the Catholic Church*, produced by the National Association of Church Personnel Administrators, and Gary Burkart's *The Parish Life Coordinator*. They provide interesting reading about the trials and tribulations of these emerging new relationships.

Will the institutional church be as strong in the next decade or two? Will the young people have the faith and church commitment of their elders? Our chapter on Post-Vatican II Catholics shows that young people have less knowledge about and commitment to specific Catholic traditional teachings than do their elders. As Davidson and Williams found in their focus groups with post-Vatican II Catholics, the commitments of these young adults have broadened to include Christian teachings and institutions more generally, not just *Catholic.*

We expect the boundaries will continue to blur, and ecumenism will come easier. Levels of support for some of the older institutional forms will probably continue to decline. At the same time, in ways still not clear to us, support for newer structural forms will eventually rise. We cannot describe the new forms except to say that they will probably be more communal and democratic than those of the past. Something of this nature is not unprecedented in Christian history.

Can the Church be an independent voice for morality and faith if its separateness and distinctness fades? Can it be countercultural in any way, or will it be one more bland version of mainline all-purpose Christianity?[4] This is the question most often voiced by critics of the integrationist vision. Our guess is that its distinctiveness does not rest entirely on its governance structure nor on its teachings. In general we do *not* believe that any change in institutional arrangements from what we have known will *ipso facto* be a downfall. To the contrary, some structural changes would enhance the Church's ability to carry out its God-given mission. A series of steps in the direction of lay participation is high on the list of desiderata and would not at all reduce the Church's ability to be prophetic and yet true to its mission. No one should believe that old forms are, for the reason of longevity alone, better. The tendency of some traditionalists to equate the Church with the clergy must, most of all, be challenged.

---

3. It is, of course, wishful thinking that the pope and bishops will make any changes in the formal authority structure in the near future, despite occasional voices suggesting such changes as female cardinals. But with the weakening of the magisterium's teaching authority generally, and with the rise of voluntary associations among Catholics of all ideological persuasions, direct voice in the decision-making process may not be an immediate priority.

4. For example, were the bishops being countercultural when they spoke out in November 1994, against the Republican Party "Contract for America" proposal to do away with most welfare benefits like AFDC? Or were they being countercultural when they opposed Proposition 187 in California in 1994? It is more likely that in these cases, the Catholic integrationists were supportive of the bishops, while the restorationists would not have been anywhere near as supportive. This raises the question just what kinds of policies and teachings may be countercultural.

The Church has abundant opportunities to be heard. Scholars in secular and Catholic universities may be encouraged to write and speak out in ways that bear witness to the Gospel while challenging church leaders to be prophetic. The bishops themselves showed signs of welcoming a more pluralistic approach to national social issues when they issued their pastorals on peace and the economy in the 1980s. And Cardinal Bernardin took a step in that direction with his Seamless Garment Consistent Life Ethic discussions. Laypersons on all sides of those issues showed an eagerness to participate that should encourage the bishops to continue the dialogue with the laity. With the current political agenda threatening harsh treatment of immigrants and their children, cutbacks in welfare, and the like, there will be no shortage of opportunities for Catholics to be heard. Prophetic voices can be heard through church organizations like the Campaign for Human Development. Recall that less than half the Catholics in our study said you could be a good Catholic without donating time and money to the poor. In the current political climate, the scene is not entirely bleak.

Restoration: A Fading Vision

A restorationist victory would mean broad-scale acceptance of autocratic leadership from the Vatican in the person of the pope. This would imply belief in the infallibility of the pope when he is speaking on matters of faith and morals. Our 1987 and 1993 surveys as well as other surveys show that less than half the Catholics accept such infallibility. Can claims to such authority be imposed? It is hard to imagine! The Catholic public's response to John Paul II's directive to end discussion on ordination of women, and his encyclical on the splendor of truth *Veritatis Splendor* were both largely ignored, received with reservations, or severely critiqued by all but the restorationists.

Any serious effort by the pope and bishops to reverse the trends described in this book would produce resistance. Without doubt the Catholic Church would survive. After all, it survived the Reformation. But the fracturing of the Church is a frightening prospect and would entail a significant loss of influence in national and international affairs.

In the near future the likelihood of anything so drastic as this is low. Most likely is a continuation of the patterns of Catholic life as we know them. A core group of Catholics, between 25 percent and 40 percent of those who define themselves as Catholic, will continue to go to Mass regularly and to contribute time and money. Active minorities on both ends of the ideological continuum will be heard. The magisterium will continue to speak out. Change will be slow. Yet some new things are happening today, which suggest that there are still areas for cooperation and consensus between the factional extremes.

Small Christian Communities and Other Groups

One development, an outgrowth of Vatican II, is the burgeoning of small Christian communities. They deserve a word of comment. There are many types today: small intentional eucharistic communities that function as parishes; small groups that meet regularly to discuss the meaning of the Scriptures for living in today's world; the RENEW program for the invigoration of parishes, which since its inception in 1976 has been adopted in more than half of the Church's dioceses; small faith groups organized around the plans of Father Arthur Baranowski (1988) for revitalizing parish life; and the Latino Base Ecclesial Communities (D'Antonio, 1992). The small faith groups organized by Father Baranowski have been started in more than sixty dioceses. In addition, there are groups that have multiple roots, generally identified with efforts to revitalize the parish.[5] Their overall orientation is integrationist.

Although most of the small faith groups operate quietly in search of spiritual renewal and outreach to the larger society, a growing number of more active groups are publicly challenging the Church. Some are old standard-bearers while others are relative newcomers. They reflect a range of integrationist views. They include Catholic Worker, *Commonweal*, the *National Catholic Reporter*, Call to Action, Women's Ordination Conference, New Ways Ministry, Catholics Speak Out, and the National Center for Pastoral Leadership.

On the other side are more conservative groups representing a range of restorationist views. They include Opus Dei, *The Wanderer*, Right to Life groups, and Catholics United for the Faith. Charismatic groups tend to be restorationist, but pockets are found at all points along the continuum.[6]

---

5. Popes Paul VI and John Paul II have given the small Christian communities movement strong support (Vandennaker, 1994). Vandennaker points out that the movement is understood to seek the revitalization of the parish, and to be under the watchful eye of the clergy from local pastors to bishops and ultimately the pope.

6. The Princeton Religion Research Center (1988) reported that 15 percent of American Catholics had participated in one or more small groups, and that about half this number, some four million Catholics, were regular participants. Catholic charismatics constituted another 6 percent of the total. These small groups are understood to provide the opportunity for " love, caring, sharing feelings of solidarity. They may persist and grow for no other reason than that they fulfill a need not met by the bureaucratic organization that is the institutional church"(D'Antonio, 1992:15; Wuthnow, 1994).

Small Groups in Large Organizations

Sociological research over many years has shown how small groups arise within larger organizations and sometimes transform the organizations. Social organization theory helps us understand the changing dynamics. Formal organizations of whatever kind have been traditionally organized around a clear-cut hierarchy and flow chart. Orders go down the chain of command, compliance reports go up. Rewards and punishments help insure compliance.

But this type of formal organization functions poorly in modern society. Gareth Morgan (1988:129) tells us why:

> The very concept of [a formal organization] as a unified system is being replaced by a network perspective on organizations. The idea of a discrete organization with identifiable boundaries is breaking down. . . . Organizations are becoming more amorphous networks of interdependent organizations where no element is in firm control. Interdependence is the key. Gone is the old-fashioned notion of hierarchy in which one member . . . directs the activities of the other members. In comes the notion of a network that must be managed as a system of interdependent stakeholders.

A hierarchical formal organization relies on a reward-punishment formula, but in the Church that formula is not working as efficiently as before. The sacrament of confession was once a mechanism of social control, but today it has almost disappeared as a regular part of Catholic life. Excommunication is even less common. With the rise of voluntary associations within the Catholic community, the lines of authority are becoming more and more tenuous. Perhaps a new form of interdependence is the key to organizational renewal. Possibly it holds promise of Church renewal. As Joseph Fichter said, the Church is being reformed from below.

The immediate future will probably feature new forms of religious vitality, like the Small Christian Communities movement. Much of the integrationist vision can be achieved without losing the next generation or silencing the Church's counterculture voice. Also some of the restorationist vision, especially on matters like abortion and sexual morality, will achieve considerable support without splitting the Church or alienating the majority of the laity. Partisans on each side need to be specific about their proposals and to refrain from doomsday rhetoric. An emphasis on process rather than abstract principle might help. Recent diocesan synods sound hopeful in this regard.

Shared Responsibility?

Is it possible to have extended discussions sponsored by the bishops about power sharing at the level of parish and diocese? What might be the consequences of allowing the laity to select priests and other professional parish leaders? In Chapter 7 we reported evidence of changes in this direction in currently priestless parishes. Why not institutionalize lay input into financial decisions at all levels, as recommended by Vatican II documents, and not just at the discretion of the pastor? Women are beginning to have access to higher positions within the Church's institutional structure; does the historical evidence really preclude their access to the roles of deaconess and priest? In the face of recent historiography, how can the Church be defended as a bastion of male control? Why not establish commissions of clergy and laypersons to review moral teachings on several issues? This would be a welcome step to a majority of the laity, and might well enhance the public dialogue over such issues as teenage pregnancy and the struggle to control the spread of AIDS.[7] Actions such as these would probably produce greater, not less, Church commitment by the laity, and they would not damage Catholic identity or the Catholic voice in the world. Organizations, for their own good, need to be reexamined from time to time to ensure their sensitivity to the "signs of the times."

Not all structural innovations will be free of problems, but a continuation of present-day practices also has problems. In the last part of the twentieth century – a time of rapid change – we cannot expect all institutional arrangements of the past to go on performing well. If they are still contributing to the God-given mission of the Church, strengthen them; if not, make adjustments to that end.

In reporting our findings, we do not presume that the lived experiences of the laity automatically or necessarily reveal either ultimate or relative truths. But neither should they be dismissed without due study and reflection. We need more willingness to relate the phenomena of lived experiences with the principles derived from natural law theory. These principles are themselves the work of the human mind, and subject to modification and change, as we have seen through history. The time is ripe for a dialogue that will provide the basis for ethical principles that reflect the love, caring, forgiveness and reconciliation that are at the heart of Jesus's teachings.

---

7. Extensive research has shown that education programs to stop the spread of AIDS have been effective, where they have enjoyed broad institutional support (Darrow, 1987; 1991).

Conclusion

Restorationists and integrationists may be encouraged by the words of Judge John Noonan as they ponder the options available. Noonan is a highly regarded scholar and judge whose book *Contraception* has been extensively cited in the great debate. He reminds us that great changes have occurred throughout the history of the Church, and things happened that were once believed impossible.

He documents how the moral teachings of the Church have changed over time, citing examples in the areas of usury, marriage, slavery, and religious freedom. Still, he acknowledges, change is resisted because it is perceived to threaten the stability of the group or organization, as well as its sense of intellectual consistency. But Noonan (1993: 676-671) urges:

> The consistency to be sought is consistency with Christ. The human desire for mental repose is not to be satisfied in this life. One can not predict future changes; one can only follow present light and in that light be morally certain that some moral obligations will never alter. The great commandments of love of God and of neighbor, the great principles of justice and charity continue to govern all development. . . . All will be judged by the demands of the day in which they live. . . . In new conditions, with new insight, an old rule need not be preserved in order to honor a past discipline.

Only through judicious reform and change can the Church, the entire People of God, maintain the strength and wisdom needed to carry out the mission to preach the Gospel to the ends of the earth.

References

Baranowski, Arthur. 1988. *Creating Small Faith Communities*. St. Anthony Messenger Press.

Briggs, Kenneth A. 1992. *Holy Siege*. San Francisco: Harper.

Burkhart, Barry. 1993. *The Parish Life Coordinator*. Kansas City, MO: Sheed & Ward.

Burns, Gene. 1992. *The Frontiers of Catholicism*. Berkeley: University of California Press.

D'Antonio, William V. 1992. "Autonomy and Community: Indicators of Change among the American Catholic Laity." *Proceedings of the Fifty-Fourth Annual Convention of the Canon Law Society of America*. Washington D.C.: The Catholic University of America.

Darrow, William. 1987. "Behavioral Changes in Response to AIDS," in U.S. Department of Health and Human Services, *Symposium International de Reflexion Sur Le Sida*: 227-230.

________ and Ronald O. Valdisseri. 1991. "New Directions for Health Promotion to Prevent HIV Infection and other STDs," in Hilary Curtis (ed.), *Promoting Sexual Health: Proceedings of the Second International Workshop on Prevention of Sexual Transmission of HIV and other Sexually Transmitted Diseases*. London: BMA: 39-54.

Dolan, Jay P. 1985. *The American Catholic Experience*. Garden City, NY: Doubleday.

Greeley, Andrew M. 1991. *Faithful Attraction*. New York: Tor Books.

_______. 1967. *The Catholic Experience*. New York: Doubleday and Co.

Laumann, Edward O., John H. Gagnon, Robert T. Michael and Stuart Michaels. 1994. *The Social Organization of Sexuality*. Chicago: University of Chicago Press.

McNamara, Patrick H. 1992. *Conscience First, Tradition Second*. Albany, NY: SUNY Press.

Morgan, Gareth. 1988. *Riding the Waves of Change: Developing Managerial Competencies for a Turbulent World*. San Francisco: Jossey-Bass.

Murnion, Phillip J. 1992. *New Parish Ministers: Laity and the Religious on Parish Staffs*. New York: National Pastoral Life Center.

Noonan, John. 1993. "Development in Moral Doctrine." *Theological Studies* 54 (December): 622-677.

Princeton Religion Research Center Report, 1988. *The Unchurched American*, 10 Years Later. The Gallup Organization: Princeton, N.J.

Schoenherr, Richard A., and Lawrence A. Young. 1993. *Full Pews and Empty Altars*. Madison: University of Wisconsin Press.

Vandennaker, John. 1994. *Small Christian Communities in the Catholic Church*. Kansas City: Sheed & Ward.

Working in the Catholic Church. 1993. Kansas City: Sheed & Ward.

Appendix

Nationwide Survey by Gallup Organization

For the *National Catholic Reporter,* May 1993

1. What is your present religion? Catholic
Other. . . . (TERMINATE)

2. I will read five items and after each, please tell me if it has strengthened your commitment to the Catholic Church, weakened your commitment to the Catholic Church, or had no effect one way or the other. If you don't know, tell me that.

	Strengthened	*Weakened*	*No Effect*	*DK/RF*
a. The Church hierarchy's teaching that artificial contraception is morally wrong.	12	33	50	5
b. The Church hierarchy's teaching that abortion is morally wrong.	38	22	36	4
c. The policy of ordaining men, but not women, to the priesthood.	15	25	56	4
d. Reports indicating that a significant number of priests have homosexual tendencies.	4	35	55	6
e. Reports indicating that a number of priests have abused children sexually.	4	50	42	5

Note: Eight hundred two (802) interviews were completed. Numbers shown are percentages. DK = don't know; RF = refused.

3. Next, I would like your opinion on several issues that involve the moral authority in the Catholic Church. In each case I would like to know who you think should have the final say about what is right or wrong. The choices are: 1) The church leaders – the pope and bishops; 2) Individuals taking church teachings into account and deciding for themselves; or 3) Individuals and leaders working together.

	Church Leaders	*Individuals*	*Both*	*DK/RF*
a. A divorced Catholic remarrying without getting an annulment.	23	38	37	2
b. A Catholic practicing contraceptive birth control.	14	57	26	3
c. A Catholic advocating free choice regarding abortion.	21	44	33	3
d. A Catholic who engages in homosexual behavior.	26	39	30	5
e. Sexual relations outside of marriage.	23	44	30	3

4. In the last five years, has your commitment to your local parish changed? Have you become more committed, less committed, or has there been no change? If you are not sure, tell me that.

More committed	22
Less committed	25
No change	50
Not sure	3

5. In the last five years, has your confidence in the American bishops changed? Have you become more confident in them, less confident, or has there been no change?

More confident	7
Less confident	29
No change	63
Not sure	1

6. In the last five years, has your confidence in the Pope and the Vatican changed? Have you become more confident in them, less confident, or has there been no change?

More confident	13
Less confident	26

No change	70
Not sure	1

7. In recent years the American Catholic bishops have written several pastoral letters. Have you heard about or read about any of the following letters?

	Yes	*No*	*Not sure*
a. The 1983 peace pastoral?	18	79	3
b. The 1985 pastoral on economic justice?	19	78	3
c. The 1992 draft pastoral letter on the role of women in the Church?	44	54	2

(IF YES ON PART C, ASK Q. 8:)
8. Do you agree, or disagree, with the bishops' decision not to publish this pastoral on women in the church?

Agree	11
Disagree	29
Not sure	4
Refused/missing	56

(ASK EVERYONE:)
9. The following statements deal with what you think it takes to be a good Catholic. Please tell me if you think a person can be a good Catholic *without* performing these actions.

	Yes	*No*	*Not Sure*
a. Without going to Church every Sunday.	73	25	2
b. Without obeying the Church hierarchy's teaching regarding birth control.	73	24	3
c. Without obeying the Church hierarchy's teaching regarding divorce and remarriage.	62	35	3
d. Without obeying the Church hierarchy's teaching regarding abortion.	56	40	5
e. Without believing in the infallibility of the Pope.	50	42	7

f. Without getting married in the Church.	61	36	3
g. Without donating time or money to help the poor.	52	44	4
h. Without donating time or money to your parish.	57	41	3
i. Without contributing money annually to the special collection for the Pope (that is, Peter's Pence).	79	18	3

10. Some people think the Catholic Church should have more democratic decision-making in church affairs that do not involve matters of faith than it has at present. Do you favor or oppose this idea . . .

	Favor	*Oppose*	*Unsure*
a. at the local parish level?	61	32	7
b. at the diocesan level?	60	27	13
c. at the level of the Vatican?	58	32	10

11. Here is a question about the American Catholic bishops. Should the American bishops become more independent or less independent from the Vatican and the Pope, in the way they run the Catholic Church in America? Or should the situation remain as it is now?

More	37
Less	11
Remain same	48
Not sure	4

12. How important is the Catholic Church to you personally?

a. the most important part of my life.	11
b. among the most important parts of my life	32
c. quite important to me, but so are many other areas of my life	40
d. not terribly important to me	10
e. not very important to me at all	6
f. not sure	1

13. How often do you attend Mass?

a. daily	2

b. at least once a week	39
c. almost every week	5
d. about once a month	18
e. seldom	20
f. never	5
g. no answer	2

14. How regularly do you pray, apart from Mass?

a. more than once a day	10
b. daily	57
c. at least once a week	14
d. occasionally	9
e. seldom	7
f. never	2
g. no answer	1

15. For each of the following areas of church life, please tell me if you think the Catholic laity should have the right to participate, or should not have the right to participate:

	Should	*Should Not*	*Not Sure*
a. Deciding how parish income should be spent.	83	13	4
b. Selecting the priests for their parish.	74	23	3
c. Making church policy about divorce.	61	35	5
d. Making church policy about birth control.	62	35	3
e. Deciding whether women should be ordained to the priesthood.	62	34	3

16. If a shortage of priests in the future required a reduction of priestly activities, some changes may occur in parish life. I am going to read a list of six changes which may occur. Would you tell me after each if you would be willing to accept it in your home parish? Tell me if it would be very acceptable, somewhat acceptable, or not at all acceptable to you.

	Very Acceptable	*Somewhat Acceptable*	*Not at all Acceptable*	*No Answer*
a. Reduce the number of Masses to less than once a week.	11	30	58	2
b. Baptisms performed only by deacons or lay officials of the Church.	26	37	35	2
c. Marriages performed only by deacons or lay officials of the Church.	20	31	47	2
d. No priest available for visiting the sick.	13	28	58	1
e. No priest available for administering Last Rites for the dying.	12	17	70	1
f. No resident priest in the parish but only a lay parish administrator and visiting priests.	15	40	42	2

17. If, due to a shortage of priests, Sunday Mass could not be celebrated, would a Communion Service led by a layperson using consecrated hosts be a satisfactory substitute for you?

Yes, on a regular basis	16
Yes, on occasion	54
Not at all	29
Don't know	1

18. Now I will read three statements about the priesthood. After each would you tell me if you agree strongly, agree somewhat, disagree strongly, disagree somewhat, or don't know.

	Agree Strongly	*Agree Somewhat*	*Disagree Somewhat*	*Disagree Strongly*	*Don't Know*
a. Since the original leaders of the Church were men, women should not be ordained to the priesthood.	19	12	22	45	2

b. It would be a good thing if married men were allowed to be ordained as priests.	47	25	7	19	2
c. It would be a good thing if women were allowed to be ordained as priests.	39	25	10	25	2

19. Now I would like you to imagine a scale from 1 to 7. At point 1 is the statement, "I would never leave the Catholic Church." At point 7 is the statement, "Yes, I might leave the Catholic Church." Where would you place yourself on that scale?

Point	*1*	*2*	*3*	*4*	*5*	*6*	*7*	*Don't Know*
	51%	10%	9%	8%	8%	3%	9%	2%

Now a few questions just for statistical purposes:

20. Are you currently married, divorced, widowed, separated, or have you never been married?

Married	54
Divorced	11
Widowed	9
Separated	3
Never married	24

21. What was the last grade or class you completed in school?

Some high school or less	20
High school graduate	39
Some college or vocational school	21
College graduate	13
Some graduate or professional school	2
Graduate or professional degree	5
Don't Know/Refused	1

22. Did you ever attend:

	Yes	*No*	*DK/RF*
a. Catholic grade school?	51	48	1
b. Catholic high school?	24	75	1
c. Catholic college?	9	90	1

23. What is your race – White, African-American, Hispanic, Asian, or some other?

White	79
African-American	5
Hispanic	13
Asian	1
Other	1
Refused	1

24. Are you now employed full-time, part-time, or not employed?

Full-time	54
Part-time	15
Not employed	31
No answer	1

25. Could you please tell me the kind of work you do?

Professional worker	16
Manager, executive, or official	7
Business owner	3
Clerical	11
Sales	5
Service	9
Skilled tradesman	12
Semi-skilled	5
Laborer	5
Full-time student	3
Retired	12
Housewife	6
Other/no answer	6

26. Is your annual *household* income before taxes:

Under $10,000 (under $192 per week)	17
$10,000 to $19,999 ($192 to $384 per week)	21
$20,000 to $29,999 ($385 to $576 per week)	18
$30,000 to $39,999 ($577 to $769 per week)	16
$40,000 to $49,999 ($770 to $960 per week)	8
$50,000 to $74,999 ($961 to $1436 per week)	9
$75,000 and over ($1437 and over per week)	5
Don't know	7

26. And what is your age? (RECORD ACTUAL AGE)

____

27. Sex:

Male	48
Female	52

Index